The Art of Sales Management
Revelations of a Goal Maker

∽∾

Michael Delaware

If, And or But
Publishing Company

Copyright © 2013 Michael Delaware

All rights reserved.

This book, or parts thereof, may not be reproduced in any form without permission from the publisher; exceptions are made for brief excerpts used in published reviews.

Published by

'If, And or But' Publishing Company
P.O. Box 2559
Battle Creek, Michigan 49016 USA
www.ifandorbutpublishing.com

ISBN-13: 978-0615903347 (If, And or But Publishing)
ISBN-10: 0615903347

This book contains clipart illustrations which were acquired by means of royalty free usage rights in 2013 and are copyright to: *GraphicsFactory.com* on pages: 1, 7, 19, 21, 24, 26, 31, 32, 35, 41, 49, 55, 71, 77, 87, 93, 101, 109, 119, 127, 133, 139, 147, 153, 159, 165, 169, 177, 179, 184, 189, 195, 199 & 213.

While attempts have been made to verify all information provided in this publication; neither the author nor the publisher assumes any responsibility for errors, omissions, or contrary interpretations of the subject matter herein. The views expressed are those of the author alone, and should not be taken as expert instruction or commands.

This book is sold with the understanding that the publisher is not engaged in rendering legal, accounting, or other professional advice. If legal or other expert assistance is required, the services of a competent person should be sought.

*This book is dedicated
to the goal makers.
New tomorrows exist because
you accepted the challenge to dream...*

Table of Contents

	Introduction	1
1.	Leadership & Teamwork	7
2.	The Many Roles of a Sales Manager	19
3.	Happiness & Goals	35
4.	Types of Goals	41
5.	Sales Meetings & Goals	49
6.	Building Teamwork	55
7.	Open Communication	71
8.	Limiting the Limitations	77
9.	Breaking Down What is Important	87
10.	Following Through	93
11.	Harmony	101
12.	Honesty & Trust	109
13.	Understanding Games	119
14.	Resilience & Continuity	127
15.	Vitality	133
16.	Continuance of Success	139
17.	Abundance & Scarcity	147
18.	The Impact of the Negative Client	153
19.	The Parachute Perspective	159
20.	Charting Progress	165
21.	Marketing & Goals	169
22.	Envisioning Outcomes	177
23.	Intention & the Goal Maker	189
24.	Summary	195
25.	Acknowledgements	199
	About the Author	201

Introduction

If you are already a sales manager, you are a goal maker, whether you know it or not. If you are entering the profession for the first time, you are, like it or not, to a greater or lesser degree, stepping into the role of a *goal maker*.

How are you faring in this role? If you are new to the job, how will you succeed? How will you train effective sales people to reach the goals you set and at the same time inspire them to also work together in harmony?

You will do this by becoming a *goal maker*, and lead them on with inspiration and vitality. You will become the personification of their visionary or goal maker so that they can be inspired to follow you. This book will teach you to do this.

I wrote this book because at some point in my journey this life I was thrust into the role of being a sales manager. Yes, I did say *'thrust'*. No matter how one tries to explain it, being a sales manager never seems to be something one originally seeks to become. At least not with any sales manager I ever met. The job sort of finds you, instead of you finding it. At least, that is how it has always happened to me and the others I consulted with.

What usually happens is one goes along ones path as a salesperson expanding upon a professional career, and the perhaps making the fateful decision to coach a newcomer who is hired and seated at the desk next to you. You coach them and they in turn become a success. Then someone taps you on the shoulder and says: *'We decided we need a sales manager, so you can do that with the others'* and then you are it.

Many years ago, this is how I began my journey as a sales manager. The job found me; I never went seeking after it. I learned from experience that one either rises to the occasion when opportunity knocks, or it eats you. Like some overzealous shark any job one is thrust into that one has no choice but to accept will eat you alive unless you rise up and conquer it. I do not like the sensation of being eaten, so I transformed into the role.

I began by assuming I knew nothing, which was the truth. I went forth from that starting point looking for answers, and found them. Some of the answers were shared to me by others, and still many more were discovered on my own through firsthand 'rolled up sleeve' experience.

I discovered the most valuable use of my time, as a sales manager, was to venture into the true understanding of people. It is a people profession, sales is. One can either recognize this, acknowledge it, or not, but it is.

Every day is a challenge to conduct a group of salespeople and keep them inspired and moving towards the goals one sets. I wanted to understand what was beneath the surface of what inspired people to perform at their best. I began setting short term, and eventually longer term goals for them to achieve and succeed better on the job. I learned that when one starts looking for these answers, and starts taking action with what one learns, one becomes ultimately their *goal maker.*

As a goal maker, one learns what works and what

doesn't. I have tried to distill, codify and include all these discoveries within this book. Throughout its writing, I have endeavored to be as concise as possible with this installment of my series on sales management, and to focus on the precise subject of being a goal maker, and all the factors that can be involved to embody that role from a sales manager's perspective.

Over the years I have always believed it is better to share wisdom rather than to hole it up and keep it to oneself. That is how discoveries get lost, and everyone becomes doomed to repeat prior mistakes as they re-learn what was already learned by others. That has been the force behind the inspiration which has driven me to write this book, as well as the preceding one: *The Art of Sales Management: Lessons Learned on the Fly.*

I think the true test of any book such as this is: Does the material *inspire you* as an author to not only write it, but are you *again inspired* when re-reading it during the editing and refining of it?

When I wrote the first book in this series, words cannot express the enrichment of spirit I felt as a writer upon completion to finally share those ideas and lessons that I carried in my heart and soul for so many years. I felt that way again while compiling the chapters in this new installment of the series.

With this book during the review and editing process, I discovered an even greater glow within it pages as I revisited each chapter to do the final revisions. The message contained in the material is rich with the magic of goal making, as well as guidance in following the blazes along a planned path towards those goals and fulfilling ones dreams. The material is timeless. It can work for any sales manager, and in any sales situation. It is important to understand that it is the message that glows, not the words from the one who wrote it.

I have drawn this material together from my many years with working with people, and caring for their success. I hope I have delivered it with the grace and finesse that the subject ultimately deserves. I have endeavored to do so, at any rate. I hope you will find your own unique inspiration within its pages.

Without further preamble, I wish you the very best on your journey in reading about my revelations from my past experiences as a goal maker. I also wish you the greatest success in applying the material to improve your own situation, and may you find your own freedom in doing so.

If you do apply it, I know you will become a

success. I can say this not because I wrote it, but because I lived everything you are about to read, and still endeavor to do so. It is the message that glows, and if it captures you as it did me, I know your heart will glow as well.

    To your success!

Leadership & Teamwork

I think I first really understood the lessons of the importance of teamwork and leadership when I was a boy playing soccer (AKA 'football' or '*futball*' for my European friends).

I was on a team when I was thirteen or fourteen years old. My brother was two years younger than I, and my mother somehow got him enrolled on the same team as mine which was eventually called the 'Renegades'. It was easier for her to have to just come to see one team play. It was on this team that I learned the painful differences between teamwork, and individualism. These lessons later followed me into my adulthood, and I was able to learn from these experiences and utilize this knowledge with others when I became a sales manager.

My mother considered it important for my brother and myself to be involved in team sports. I wanted to play American football, but she was concerned about the injury potential, and so enrolled my brother and me in a youth soccer team. I soon learned that I was a horrible soccer player. My team consisted of kids that had been playing for a number of years, and this was my first experience with the sport. I was never much into sports that involved continual running and running like soccer required. I liked football because I usually played the defensive line, and there was not that much running required in that position on the few teams I played on.

The soccer coach assured us all that he would treat us all equally and fairly, but that soon did not seem to be the case. One kid in particular by the name of Terry was a natural superstar in this sport. Terry could drive a soccer ball down the field, cut right when you cut left, and essentially zigzag his way effortlessly towards making a shot on goal. Even the seasoned players looked like a newbie around this kid, and I looked like a complete inept idiot whenever I had to do some drill against him. Many times Terry had me all spun around after I tried to defend against him, and he made most anyone look like an amateur.

      To top it all off, not only was Terry good, he knew he was. Oh yes, he was a real class act about it too. He carried an attitude with him where he thought he had the right to be critical of everyone, and belittle them for simply not being as good a player as he was. This attitude he turned up a notch against me whenever he had the opportunity. I was an inferior soccer player, and it being my first year, he made damn sure that I knew it should be my last, even though I was older than he was. He wanted to establish that he knew I sucked, and did not waste any opportunity in expressing his viewpoint whenever I was gathered around my other team mates. This made for a very warm and friendly atmosphere, I can assure you.

      Despite his vociferous and critical attitude, I must admit I admired Terry. He had everything in terms of talent. He could out-run everyone on the team. He could maneuver the ball, and he could shoot and he could score like a rocket shot out of a cannon from almost every acrobatic position imaginable.

      I, on the other hand was quite pathetic as an

athlete in this sport. I was at best a slow to average runner. I tripped over the soccer ball when I tried to run and kick it down the field, and whenever I was in a position to score my feet never seemed to be able to find the ball. Terry and I were polar opposites in terms of athleticism.

Perhaps the only thing that kept me from getting cut from the team was the fact that my brother was an average and upcoming player, and our mother had a large Chevy 'Carry-All' station wagon and had agreed to be one of the drivers of the team to games. If it had not been for this last one, I think I would have been cut from the team. My younger brother, on the other hand, would have probably been allowed to remain on the team, as he had played for another soccer team the prior season, and had developed some skill.

It is always easy to look back at this sort of thing, and see things you were oblivious to in your youth. When I recall those times, I know I was completely naive to all of these things until I grew to adulthood and was able to examine them in retrospect. Regardless, I stayed on the team and was present at all of the games we played. Most of the time I rode the bench or was played as a rotational player in the fullback position along with a few other kids that were kind of in my category.

Terry on the other hand was a starting forward in every single game, and he was our teams lead score master. He made goalies look like chumps, over and over again.

It was around the second week of the season when we had played approximately six games, and won four of them that a new kid arrived and was allowed to join the team. We had been practicing two weeks before the season started, so we were about three weeks into being together as a team.

The new kid's name was Laszlo, and he was almost a foot taller than the rest of us. Laszlo was from Yugoslavia and had been playing soccer since he sprung from the womb. His natural and graceful ability with a soccer ball was like watching a ballerina in a grand performance. He did not speak very much English at first, but his talent spoke without words. Laszlo soon turned the notch up on Terry because it was clear to all that he was no longer the best player on the team. To top it all off, Laszlo was a friendly and kind kid with a great attitude.

The coach adopted a strategy to win which consisted of playing Terry and Laszlo as the two forwards, and the rest of us just filled up the roster and ran up and down the field. These two kids controlled the ball, and scored on these other teams like crazy. The Renegades soon moved up the rankings, and after many wins created mainly by Terry and Laszlo, we went to the play offs.

During most of these games, my mother drove the team, and my brother and I frequently rode the bench. We would sit on the sidelines on a soccer ball sometimes when there were no other benches, and hope with eager anticipation that we would be allowed to enter the game. More often than not, my brother was selected to go in over myself, and if either of us were played for any longer than a few plays it was because we were so far ahead in the score that the coach did not care, or it was a mere oversight on his part as he was busy calling in instructions to Terry and Laszlo.

It was during these play offs that I soon learned the most important lessons about team work that I ever experienced. As our team reached the play offs, we continued to play good. We beat other teams, or should I say, Terry and Laszlo did. I was caught up in the euphoria that my team was winning, as one can so often do in ones youth that I overlooked the growing resentment I had for the coach because he would not let me participate equally. I felt the same vibes from my mother when she would watch the games knowing her sons were not being played. I felt it from the other mothers too, who had their kids benched repeatedly for the *Terry and Laszlo show*.

Then something amazing happened. We reached the semi-finals, and with one more win we would be in the State finals for our division. Every kid on the team could see that trophy, and was looking forward in anticipation of the win. Nobody could beat Terry and Laszlo. Or could they?

Our record was something ridiculous like 35 or 40 wins to 3 or 4 losses. This duo was certainly an incredible deadly combination. Despite our inherent knowledge that it was largely the doing of just these two kids, we all felt we were a part of some future glory soon to be had.

I still remember to this day that final semi-final game. I can only remember bits and pieces of all the others games that season, but this one I remember almost every play. It hangs with me to this day. It was a wake-up call of understanding, and perhaps became one of the most important lessons of my youth.

We were facing a team called the 'Shamrocks' and we knew very little about them as they came from the other side of Arizona from where we were. They turned out to not only good, they were great. Their style of play consisted of using every team player, and everyone passed the ball. Each player knew their positions, and they moved together like clockwork.

The amazing fact was they passed the ball at least 5 or 6 times to different players as they marched down the field. They were so precise; one could see they had practiced this over and over again. They had no single super star players per se, and one could even say individually they were all somewhat mediocre in terms of talent. However, what they did have was teamwork and they destroyed us. They tore our defenses to pieces, and robbed Terry and Laszlo so many times when they tried to drive down the field. They made Terry and Laszlo look like miniature tornadoes spinning around trying to see where the ball went because by the time it was stolen, it was passed, passed and passed far down the field in the opposite direction. It was almost comical, yet sad at the same time.

Despite all of Terry and Laszlo's star power play, we were defeated by a score of 8-2. They played like a unified organism and were impossible to beat. Our team had the flaw that we were merely a two man team, and although our two guys were talented, we were incomplete.

The Shamrocks on the other hand played

together, and no one was trying to outshine the other. They were consistent throughout their play, and moved the ball down the field like clockwork. Their defense was equally consistent, and they would run cross patterns that we had never seen to steal the ball from Terry and Laszlo, and pass it out of their reach right on down the field. Despite our best efforts, they sliced us apart and exposed us for all of our weaknesses. Our own lack of teamwork destroyed us.

So from this experience I learned the valuable lesson of teamwork. Conversely I also was shown an important example in lack of leadership by our coach. Our couch did not seek to build us into a team the minute he saw the second star arrive on the scene in Laszlo. He simply let the two of them take over the offense, and do what they wanted. His coaching became a lot of switching the other kids in the back field, often leaving Terry and Laszlo in for the entire game without a break. He turned the team into a two person show, and the rest of us became useless extras. He set goals for himself, based on these two kids talent, but was not a goal maker for the group as a whole.

His lack of leadership showed in all of its flaws the moment we faced the Shamrocks. He began screaming at us kids like an insane maniac throughout the Championship game. He even screamed at Terry and Laszlo and put them into tears at one point. The truth was revealed in this final episode. There was no team, because the one trusted to provide leadership had failed to build one. When we finally faced a true team, we were destroyed in the field of contest and crushed like insects.

So the lessons I was able to extract from this experience and relate it to sales management was that one can certainly have talent come your way as a manager, but one cannot overlook the importance of utilizing all the other players and continue building a team.

Riding the talents of a few will ultimately result in failure, and every flaw that you have will be exposed when faced with a true match. Terry and Laszlo were talented, but they also became our flaw simply because they were just two kids. The other team had their full complement of players, and thus we were outnumbered, even though in body we had the same number on the field.

So it becomes a lesson in the responsibility of a manager to build those he manages into a team, and drive them with common goals. There will always be the occasional talent that can tempt one with complacency, but a leader should never give into this temptation. To focus on the extreme talent in a few, is to overlook the emerging talent in the many others.

This lesson with the Shamrocks taught me that when a true leader leads a group, even a team with marginal emerging talent can defeat the other team with the better record and pedigree of superstars if they have teamwork.

Thus we learn when we examine this kind of scenario that the important elements of success do not necessarily require great players, but they do require great teamwork. In fact one can go so far as to say real 'players' are secondary to the structure of a team. However, a group of sincere dedicated players, regardless of talent are more valuable than a single great player. Then 'great players' are therefore lower on the list below a 'team' and 'players', as a 'team of players' will run circles around a few talented ones every time.

1) Team Work

2) Players

3) Great Players

This book is about discovering for yourself as a sales manager that you have the responsibility to lead, and become a goal maker for your team. It is written to help you find players, and build them into great players, but first and foremost your direction should be to build a team. Teams win against competition. Individuals will do not endure long when faced with the competition of a true team.

This book is more than a lesson on the importance of teamwork; it is about leadership and being the goal maker that you are entrusted to be whenever you take on the role of leading others.

The Many Roles of a Sales Manager

In the arena of sales, who really is the manager and what is his or her role in the grand scheme of things? Do they know what their role is?

Let's explore some of these roles further. What would our ideal sales manager do, see and feel on a day to day basis? What would be his or her actions, and what more importantly would be their overall results expected?

When we take into consideration all of these things, and ponder them for a moment, we see that there is a great deal to the role of a sales manager. There are many challenges, and many potential aspects to the job. Every company one works for will have their own unique struggles, personalities and dynamics.

It becomes more than just overseeing the actions of others in the course of a day, and counting the sales at the end of a day. No, most certainly it is much, much more.

THE SALES MANAGER AS AN OPERATIONS MANAGER

Looking through the eyes of our sales manager, we see that as a basic routine, he or she must keep the operation there. They must keep the lights one, the computers running and the phone lines working in a sales environment for sales to function at all.

There are also other elements like support staff and supplies. Secretaries to direct the incoming call volume to the right people. Following routine promotional actions, and seeing they are adhered to so that the calls continue to come in. Making sure the environment is friendly and inviting to whomever should stop by.

All of these things could be listed under simply

the heading of 'operations' within any sales environment yet are vital to the group success. These basic operations are what makes it possible to sell, and could be said to be the foundation of the operation that must be laid before the rest can be built. However, one can still sell without all of these things, and it is how organizations quite often start out.

Many such activities start out selling from a small office, or from someone's kitchen table, and then growing over time to larger quarters, etc. Operations could perhaps better be defined as 'functions of group existence' if one really wanted to get technical. However, a sales manager concerns him or herself with operations only so that the sales activity can get on with things.

THE SALES MANAGER AS A CONDUCTOR

In any business, the manager is also much like a conductor of an orchestra. They direct the movements of the people under their direction, through policies and instruction. They make decisions about day to day operations, including personnel, policy, and finance. Their job is to maintain orderly production, achieve short term goals and make quotas. They achieve this through the people they direct, and in this case it is with the professionals we call 'salespeople' which are the scope of this book.

A good general definition of the word manager in a dictionary defines it as "*A person responsible for controlling or administering all or part of a company*". The keywords here are of course '*responsible*' and '*control*'.

If one is not willing to assume responsibility, one will not have much success. Likewise, if the person in the role of manager is weak on his or her ability to control things, they will do very poorly in controlling a group on a day to day, week to week or even a monthly basis.

The sales manager is therefore one who maintains the orderly progression towards a group goal, factoring in personalities, levels of skill and difficulty of all those under his or her charge. They have to be a responsible person, and have to be able to control others to reach its goal. That goal usually is greater and greater sales production at a steady pace, week after week, throughout the year.

Some weeks are better than other ones, and certainly not every week is progressively better than the prior. There are ups and downs in any sales activity, but a sales manager's primary job is to see to it that there are more ups than downs. Too many down weeks makes for a declining sales income and eventual collapse of the company if it goes beyond a certain point.

It is that understanding and ability that a sales manager must achieve in order to keep the overall activity progressing along a path towards continued survival for the company. There are many factors that can come into play that a sales manager must be in control of to a greater or lesser degree in order to bring about prolonged success. This book is about just that.

In this book, I will be elaborating on the subject of goals as it relates to a manager, and how these goals and his or her understanding of the subject empower him or her, and the group.

Other definitions of 'managers' include: "*An individual who is in charge of a certain group or subgroup in a company entrusted with performing certain tasks for that company. A manager usually has a group of people reporting to them to accomplish such tasks."*

So we see that the role of manager also embraces terms such as 'trust' and 'performance' in its definition. It also includes 'people' who work for him or her to help accomplish those tasks, and bring about performance and trust.

THE SALES MANAGER AS A PROBLEM SOLVER

Many times a sales manager must solve problems for others that are seemingly unrelated to the activity at hand. Sales staff with personal life problems will sometimes come to one in this position, because 'no one' else ever seems to understand their troubles. Over time in such a position, one will grow accustomed to dealing with all sorts of personnel problems, both personal and professional.

Being able to maintain a position as a '*problem solver*' while at the same time remaining keen to the task of the overall activity is important. Being patient, and understanding and helpful builds trust. It also can build confidence in one as their manager if one is simply willing to listen when they need help.

In many cases, one will find that it is not so much a matter of solving the problem for them. Sometimes it is just listening to them explain it to you and acknowledging that you understand what they are dealing with that helps them solve it for themselves..

Not every problem has an immediate answer. No solution is always the only solution, or the best. As a sales manager I learned that it is more important to guide those struggling with a personal problem towards their own answer, rather than trying to solve it for them directly. Knowing which scenario requires what approach is a matter of judgment at the time it occurs.

THE SALES MANAGER AS A BACK UP PERFORMER

Have you ever been involved in a stage production, and had to make a last minute replacement? I once saw the lead actor in a production of the Christmas Carole walk off in a fit of anger two weeks before the opening night, and never return. The new Scrooge had to learn his lines in a crash course, in order to pull it off.

The role of a sales manager is often one of stepping in as a back-up. Not just when someone leaves, or has a day off or is out sick. No, it can be just when a place it too crowded and a second hand is needed to handle the volume. This second hand needs to be impartial and respectful of whose sale it is, and whose commission. Not every sale happens in sequential order. There are many times when they happen all at once, and returning customers can converge on a single sales person all at once. This is a role where the sales manager often steps in and offers assistance to service the customer, and help maintain order.

A sales manager can also serve as a back up as mentioned whenever a sales person is not present who is dealing with a particular client. They can also take over when the going gets rough, and salvage a sale that would otherwise have been lost. There are many roles a sales manager can play in the 'back-up performer' mode. All of them are in the effort to help maintain order, and achieve the group goal of success.

THE SALES MANAGER AS A BUFFER

When there is trust and responsibility we have freedom to carry on with one's own vision for their area or team, and thus if the company is run by entrusting and responsible people at the top, a sales manager position can offer a great deal of freedom to operate. One can often create the job as one would wish, as long as there is performance, production and improvement in the area.

So thus we see that a sales manager must have a stable group of people above them in order to create a stable group of people below them and accomplish their goals.

When one is infested with a capricious, corrupt or unpredictable management above the sales manager, the task can become even more difficult as one will constantly be rebuilding. Policies of such a senior management often tear apart that which one creates. Often they do it with a misdirected idea that they must remain in control at all times, and thus change the rules constantly, creating disharmony within the ranks of those below them. They also do this by injecting unpredictable policies, creating uncertainty in the entire operation.

When one is at the receipt end of such an upper management operating basis, one never knows what will happen next. Personnel are randomly fired; the wrong people are hired to perform vital functions of which the sales staff depends upon, and so forth. It can be a more ego driven style of management, rather than one built upon intelligent observation and verifiable facts. We have all seen or heard of the existence of companies where someone gets promoted not on merit, but on familial connections. One can never expect much in the way of wisdom from a management style such as that.

One week the sales staff is permitted to sell a product one way, the next it is forbidden with no logical explanation given as to why. The following week that restriction is relaxed, and a new restriction or policy is introduced that tries to solve one problem but recklessly creates another through these kinds of capricious senior management decisions. Such an environment can be crazy for a sales manager, or any manager to operate in or under. One often takes on the role of 'buffer' between those that one depends on to produce, and those that create the madness.

Here is an example: I once worked in a book distribution center, selling published materials. The organization also sold study courses along with the books that accompany them. For years the income from both of these was combined and reported each week, as this was what company policy had been. Then an order came down that the two needed to be separated and reported separately from there on out.

Then a few days later an order was sent to backdate all the records for twelve months, and report these as separate so they could see the statistics of these two.

During the process the sales managers were reprimanded for having not done this previously, despite the fact that existing company policy prior to that point was that they were to be reported combined. The negative connation was communicated that it should have been done the other way despite the fact that the computerized system for reporting this had no other option to do this.

Crazy orders and communications from above can cause an activity to shrink, and send those working in it into circles of frustration. As a manager, one learns to become the buffer between upper management in these situations, and those working below them to contain the insanity it conveys. However, is can make it a very lonely job at times when one is in such a situation, and required to do so in an effort to maintain order.

As a sales manager, I must confess that I have broken many a telephone receiver and shouted at many a computer screen when such incidents occurred. However, I learned that it was better to not pass along the frustration to others, as it served no good, but only contaminated the environment and perpetuated the insanity.

Imagine the idea of someone pouring ink on you. It is better to just deal with it, rather than jump in a swimming pool with others and get it all over them too. As tempting as it may be to share the misery, I have learned that restraint was always the more prudent answer in these situations. However, it does make one wonder at times.

THE SALES MANAGER AS A VISIONARY

When one is given the freedom to carry on, it opens a lot of possibility. Whenever one is placed in a position as a sales manager, and allowed to be as creative as one wants in the position, it will soon be easy to envision the future. One has to be willing of course to look, and break out of the comfort zone to see that there can be much more than there is. If one can do this, then they can embrace the idealism of the group, and project where is can go.

A sales manager must see ahead for the entire activity and in doing so he or she becomes a visionary to a greater of lesser degree. The size of the vision does not matter. What is most important is that they can see into the future, which puts them one step beyond just functioning in the 'here and the now'. It places them squarely into understanding that tomorrow can always be better.

The more one practices seeing into the future, the greater one will envision tomorrow. If one can see a small gain, then one can see a slightly larger one, and then a larger one. Soon one will be seeing even greater gains, and mountains of gains to be had for the group as a whole. In doing so, one then crosses over into the next most important step in their growth as a sales manager.

THE SALES MANAGER AS A GOAL MAKER

Setting goals for a group goes hand in hand with envisioning the future. One must first be able to see what the possibility of the future could be, before one can effectively set goals to arrive there. So I have always considered that the visionary step was equal importance to what followed, which was being a goal maker.

The book is going to expound upon the subject of goal making and achieving goals from many angles and directions. To fully understand the possibilities that can happen with solid goal making is in itself a revelation. Characterized often by a great dynamic leader leading the charge for a group, the concept of a goal maker is often emboldened with the greatness of leadership. However, it is much simpler and more basic than that, which is the scope of this book. Anyone can become a goal maker without having to lead the charge.

One will learn there are both a mechanical aspect of setting a goal, and also a spiritual side to it as well. It is akin to a duality as expressed in Taoism as the yin and yang. Complementary forces not opposed, interacting to form a whole greater than their separate parts. It is the indivisible whole of the successful actions of a goal maker.

The magic of getting a group to embrace the goal maker, and the vision is what this book is about. That is the true revelation of a goal maker that I wish to share.

Happiness & Goals

There is a magic about goals. It is not what one thinks, however, that it is the mere existence of goals that is magical. Nor is it the accomplishment of them. No, the true magic is the ride towards those goals. *That is the true happiness of living.*

As a *goal maker*, one must ascertain what the best strategic goals for the organization are, and all the sub-goals along the way. However the *true happiness* is not in how great these individual goals are, but the process of moving towards them that is where the happiness of living exists. One can have a great goal drawn out in detail posted on a bulletin board somewhere, and look at this for motivation every day if one wishes. However, if one is not moving towards that goal, there will be unhappiness.

It is a fact of life that happiness lays not in possession, but in action. It is the action of moving towards goals that is the true magic of it all. One can have the goal to buy a new car, or even a new house. They can make all the motions to do it, and finally get the end result.

Throughout the process of hunting for the new house or car is they experience the excitement and enthusiasm of living. It is fun, and exciting! Then once one makes the final purchase, and drives that car for a week or lives in the house for a month, the magic kind of wears off doesn't it? Have you ever experienced this?

That is what is important to understand about goals. Goals serve as the marker, or objective down the road that one is heading for that is so absolutely necessary. They chart the progress of the journey as they are obtained, but they in themselves are not where happiness lies. The true happiness is the journey getting there. That is living.

Once one comes to understand this as a sales manager, one can see the impact of this in others that one is in charge of. Are they not happy? When one understands this, one will know why they are not happy. It is not that they do not have goals. No, it is that they are not moving towards them or any goal!

With this knowledge, one can understand how to sort out any salesperson that is in trouble. It is not that they are necessarily bad in skill or technique. Everyone of course can always benefit from training, and can improve in these areas. The true nature of the problem lies in the fact that they are not personally progressing towards a goal of any kind.

As a sales manager, one needs to sit down with all of their salespeople individually at least once a month and ask them about their goals. Get them to see the difference between the obtaining of a goal, and the journey. When they realize that it is not the goal itself that is happiness, but the journey, then they can suddenly recognize for themselves what is happening in not only their life as a salesperson, but in their life outside the office too.

Whenever someone is not doing well, it is often attributed to a 'lack of happiness'. This 'lack of happiness' is often wrongly assigned as *'Oh, this person needs to get a life'* or *'they just are never happy and that is how they are'*. This is a falsehood. People are unhappy in life simply because they are not moving towards a personal goal of their own design. One needs to have goals in life, and get their life in order to move towards those goals to be truly happy.

Here is a suggested exercise for anyone to use. Sit down alone and write out the answers to the following questions for yourself personally:

- *What things do you want to have in life?*
- *Where would you like to be in your career in 1 year, 2 years or 5 years?*
- *What have you always wanted to accomplish for yourself?*
- *If you could change one thing in life right now, what would that be?*
- *Is there something that you have always wanted to do? What is it?*
- *What would be the best thing that could ever happen to you?*
- *Draw up similar questions on your own to really dissect one's own personal goals and*

> *get them sorted out. Write them down. Post them where you can look at them. Adjust them as your interests change. Then ask yourself: What steps do I need to make right now today to move towards those goals? What steps do I need to make tomorrow?*

This becomes a daily routine. Taking steps towards your goals. They can by baby steps, or grand full extended stride steps. What is important is not how big the steps are, but that you are making steps towards your goals. If you can accomplish this in your daily routine, you will find that you are happy with living. Your own personal attitude will change about life in general. You will feel that sense of accomplishment daily and you won't be afraid to set yourself higher and higher goals.

The main reason people do not set themselves higher and higher goals is not that they cannot obtain them, but it is that they have had no prior success in moving towards any goal. They have completely omitted the motion required to experience happiness! This can be for a lot of reasons. One can have chosen a goal that was not accurate, or what they truly wanted, or the goals were enforced upon them by someone else, which are the most common reasons. One must be able to choose, and embrace their own goals or they will not move towards them.

Thus these individuals who have failed at goals have not experienced enough happiness to motivate them to continue. This also explains why people abandon goals. It is not that the goal was necessarily bad or impossible, but that they did not move towards it. They made no forward progress and thus never tasted the sweet nectar of happiness that comes with the motion towards goals.

So if you want to experience happiness in living, set some goals. Make sure they are your own goals and that you are feeling good about them and you are willing to embrace them. Once you have done that, chart out your daily routine in life to make steps towards them, and you will begin to feel happy in life and you will have the magic formula of living in your hands.

Types of Goals

As a sales manager one is ultimately placed in a position of being a goal maker at some point. One is often entrusted by the company to direct the discipline and stay focused with the team to achieve the profit motivations of the company at large. These are typically defined as one's ability to achieve goals, and ultimately are the performance indicators of a successful sales manager.

Setting goals to meet the broader goals of the company are an important aspect of the job. One in fact becomes a goal maker for goal makers. One must develop a long and short range sales plan to follow in order to accomplish this, which becomes the daily strategy to accomplish these overall goals.

The results from ones actions as a sales manager are often recorded in the form of sales reports to upper management. In larger companies, sales reports are often required by investors, partners and sometimes the government, depending on what type of company you are in. You are in effect satisfying the requests and desires of all the stakeholders in the company, so one should come to realize that having some knowledge of how to set goals as well as become a goal maker is of value.

There can be many types of goals to consider. For the sake of simplicity, I am going to focus on just four main categories of goals: *Long range goals, quarterly goals, short term goals*, and *special inventory or product sales goals.*

LONG RANGE GOALS

Long range goals typically are in terms of years. They can include goals for the coming year, or the next five years or the decade. There are management goals, market share goals and monetary goals within the scope of long range goals.

Management goals can consist of what new areas

or territories the company is going to expand into. These commonly are outside the control of the average sales manager. However, they need to be known about by the sales manager as it can be a motivating and inspirational effect of sales, and helpful to sales people to know and look forward to the future.

Market share goals consist of putting your company product into the hands of consumers on a larger and larger scale as time progresses. The greater market share, the greater ease it is to sell the product, and the more rapid growth one can expect in sales. Market share can be driven by company marketing and advertising, but it is always flanked with the actions of the sales department.

Monetary goals are typically marked out and given to a sales manager as targets to achieve quarterly or annually by management. Sometimes these totals are given each month.

It is a wise sales manager that understands these goals, and then sets their goals to exceed these each month with the sales team.

If one plays for exceeding the goal required by ones superiors, then most of the time even if you fall a little short on the higher goal you set, you are still meeting company expectations.

QUARTERLY GOALS

Quarterly goals can be both monetary and inventory related. In terms of inventory, it can be number of units remaining in inventory at the close of the quarter, etc. The sales manager typically has the goal of not only achieving monetary goals on a quarterly basis, but also reducing inventory to keep new inventory moving in.

These of course go hand in hand most of the time; however, a company that sells both service related products that are intangible, along with ones that are tangible can lose sight of the important of moving inventory if they focus too much on service alone. Therefore quarterly goals are sometimes divided into different categories to reflect the needs of the company.

To achieve quarterly goals, a sales manager needs to be able to think in terms of three months of production or 12 weeks. There must be a plan in place to break down this one goal into at last 12 individual parts, and factor in adjustments for seasons, holidays, and all the other variables that can go into a quarter.

SHORT TERM GOALS

Short term goals are typically set for a given month in the year, and of course there are twelve. Each month ideally would build upon greater success than the one before. These are often called monthly goals. One can also have, and should operate with as a main function weekly goals every week.

It is in these weekly goals that the ultimate success of the sales manager comes into play. It is easy to shake off a bad week, and move on and create a huge turn around the following week. It is much harder to do that on a monthly approach alone. One should manage tediously on a weekly basis, and use the monthly, quarterly and annual goals as guideposts to keep one on track in their day to day planning.

Weeks are best played in installments of a game, and there will be more on games later in this book. Making each week unique and fresh, and giving the sales people ability to bring to closure for them on a good or bad week every seven days is quite therapeutic.

Short term goals are the bread and butter of a sales manager's daily existence. How well your week is going is what guides your day to day actions. Is a sales person who did well last week suddenly having trouble this week? What changed? It is easier to look at changes and correct them in the short term to keep on track for a goal than the let them fall apart and take forever to rebuild by waiting to the end of a month to make changes or adjustments.

One learns that success lies in managing on a short term, as opposed to waiting for the month to expire. This becomes necessary to one's survival as a sales manager. Charting progress and inspecting production of the members of your team is easier to gauge on a short term, and by comparing their past progress on a long term by operating on a weekly sales basis.

Some would argue that a sales manager should be goal setting on a monthly basis, but I would argue that this essentially means that the sales manager is only accountable for a positive production twelve times a year. I would much rather see them accountable for 52 weeks in a year, as it is much easier to make corrections that impact the long term if one is charting progress on a shorter term as well as a long term.

SPECIAL INVENTORY OR PRODUCT SALES GOALS

A specialized classification of goals is the goals related to specialized areas of the company, usually in regards to inventory and the introduction and retiring of products. As a sales manager, these types of goals can get interjected into the daily operation throughout the course of a given year. They may have advanced planning and then again they may not.

Sometimes products are discontinued from production. There can be many reasons for this. It can be caused by sudden political problems in the exporting country of origin. It can be caused by the mere replacement of older models with newer ones, or even the discovery of latent defects in existing products that requires them to be discounted, sold off and discontinued. Sometimes the task of liquidating this inventory or product line falls into the hands of the sales manager to direct the sales staff to sell, sell and sell until they are gone.

These become specialized goals that align with financial goals, but always have the pressure of the time clock to liquidate them before too much time makes matters worse. So these specialized goals can get added to the timeline of the weekly, quarterly and annual goals, and must be carefully executed so as not to distract from the long range ones in effect.

48 — The Art of Sales Management

Sales Meetings & Goals

Whenever a sales manager or executive charts out some group goals, it is always a good idea to use the sales meeting to mull over the goals with the team involved in accomplishing them. In fact, in the creation process of goals, one could even allow the sales team themselves to create their own goals together. This can be an essential part to building teamwork, and getting all players on board to shoulder the effort of the task at hand.

As a sales manager, one just needs to make sure the goal is challenging, but not below expectations or to over the top where they will all feel like they lost before they start. Setting a goal too low can of course make for too easy a contest, and reversely setting a goal too high can make it to unreal and the result is apathy. So with using a sales meeting to accomplish part of your task of goal making, it is important to understand these variables.

It is best to run through the list of goals for the month, quarter only at sales meetings and set the company goal oneself to place the long term goal for them as the ultimate measuring stick. Then you can ask them these questions about the goals they set for themselves and as a team in the sales meeting:

- *Does this goal you are setting track with the year end goal?*
- *Is the goal too unreal?*
- *Is the goal challenging?*
- *Is the goal too easy?*
- *Do you feel you can make this goal?*
- *Do you feel it is possible to exceed this goal?*

- *Will you secretly try to beat this goal yourself?*

- *What would be the best reward for meeting the goal of _____?*

- *Who would you have to become to achieve that goal?*

- *Can you be that salesperson?*

Asking questions like this can yield a lot of valuable information for a sales manager. However, the purpose of this exercise is not to gather information. When one is goal making in a meeting with a team of sales people, one is trying to inspire their imagination, and get them to make the reality of these goals a part of their own universe.

A sales meeting is a vehicle every sales manager should use to train, gather information and realign goals with the group. It becomes the catalyst for achieving goals, and to omit a weekly sales meeting with a team one manages is to allow too much time to enter into the equation. Time without direction will drift one off course, and sales goals will become harder to reach. It is much easier to make adjustments, correct and rekindle goals and purposes to achieve them through regular meetings.

The task of using goal setting and adjusting in a sales meeting along with training exercises as discussed in my earlier book is to make sure salespeople can leave the meeting embracing the vision for themselves, and feel inspired to take on the challenge. This is the most important outcome, and the least is the information that one gleans from the exercise. The information can be revealing and important, of course, but the embracing of the goals and the kindling of imagination is what is of most senior importance in this regard.

A team that embraces a team goal will shoulder the responsibility of seeing that it is met, and thus the burden of the final outcome is shared among the group. Too often a sales manager falls into the idea that they alone need to see that the goal is achieved, and this is not the case.

The magic of being a goal maker is getting others to be inspired to meet those goals, and share the responsibility so that a group people carry a portion of the success together and together as a whole, greater things can be accomplished. In this way, larger and greater goals can be made by simply expanding the team and dividing up responsibility. It is teamwork inspired by the goal maker that make the impossible happen, and the greatest goals to be achieved.

The best tool for a sales manager to do this with is to use the sales meeting to one's own advantage, and train, educate and inspire the salespeople on ones team to make the goals one sets a reality.

Building Teamwork

How does one take a group of isolated individuated individuals and form them into a cohesive unit, one that is commonly called a 'Team'? There are many, many different philosophies on teaching teamwork, and perhaps the most notable is the catchphrase "There is no 'I' in 'TEAM'" There is a lot of basic truth in that message, and it does convey a togetherness that embodies teamwork.

However, how can you truthfully look at a group and know you have a team? Webster's offers two unique definitions on this:

1) A group of people constituting one side in a contest or competition.

2) A group of people working together in a coordinated effort.

Let's juxtapose these two individual definitions for a moment. The first one defines a 'contest' and 'competition'. The second covers the coordinated effort of people working together. So with definition number one, one must consider this from the point of view of two opposing forces engaged in a test of skill or a game. With definition number two, it defines coordinated actions of a group working towards a common goal, expressed as teamwork.

In sales, there is always an element of 'us versus them' in day to day existence and operation. It is you against the 'competition'. However, as I discussed in my first book on this subject: *The Art of Sales Management: Lessons Learned on the Fly* one has to really come to an understanding on what the competition is and who they are in fact. Are they the other competitor who has a product similar to yours? If you are a car dealer, is it the other dealership right down the street?

Certainly it is, as they are competing for that individual who is in the market for a car, and they are shopping. There is no doubt about the validity of that argument. The person who has entered the frame of mind that they are going to buy a car will eventually arrive at that goal, and there is a competition in the field of sales to make sure that they make their purchase through you and not through you competitor.

However, it is too narrow a focus to just factor this alone into the consideration of the subject of 'competition'. To simply say that the dealership down the street is your competition, leaves you somewhat defenseless when you discover you lost a sale to another company, and you customer spent their down payment on a new boat or on camping equipment instead. To exist with the idea that your only competition is the other dealership selling the same model of car that you are selling is very narrow indeed when one looks at that example.

The wakeup call that every sales person eventually needs to receive is that universal discovery of who the competition truthfully is. We have entered a global age in the world of commerce. Any individual with a laptop computer, ipad or iphone can make purchases from anywhere. They can buy a product sitting on a subway in Manhattan, and on the rooftop of a condominium in suburbia if they choose, all from a hand held device.

Certainly, larger purchases are often made in person, and face to face with a salesperson. However, it is naïve to be of the idea anymore that the person sitting in front of you has come to you to experience the first presentation on your product.

It is equally naïve to be of the idea that that same person has not been looking at competitive products, or even spending their money on something else entirely different. All one really knows when they first make contact with a prospect these days is that there is a desire or interest to buy. That is all. What they will buy, and from whom they will buy is yet to be decided. This is where salesmanship enters into the equation. This is the skill of the salesperson that will be either the conqueror or the conquered.

So the competition is more that just the business down the street selling the same model as yours. It is more than just a business selling a similar product as yours. It at its fundamental basic is: anywhere your prospect will spend his money other than through your company.

When one embraces this view, it opens a lot of doors. The salespersons viewpoint shifts once they make this realization. Their pitch of their product becomes much more broad in nature, but precise in its accuracy. One suddenly is not just selling in differences of your product against another similar one, but one is selling value, and benefits at a whole new level. This is where it is necessary to understand this definition of teamwork, and really define the competition.

The competition is: *Anywhere your customer will spend his or her dollars other than with you.*

That is it in its most simple form.

So to build teamwork on this, one must address it with each individual salesperson one on one to make sure they really understand this concept, and know it as a fundamental basic in which they can build their skill upon. Then, one must challenge the group to become a team with this vision as well.

How does one accomplish this? Through the second definition given above: "A group of people working together in a coordinated effort." It is the sales manager's job to accomplish this 'coordinated effort'.

One of the best ways to accomplish this is through sales meetings as I discussed in depth in my earlier book. However, there is more to this that I will go into here, which is the specific series of drills that one can use to help invite this concept of 'teamwork' to set in, and help them gain insight together on the subject what a 'coordinated effort' really is.

I call these drills *'Team Coordination and Learning Drills'* and I used to use these often when I was working with a staff of about 40+ people in a Stained Glass Window and Door Manufacturing company I owned and operated with my business partners in the Atlanta, Georgia area in the 1980's and 90's.

We had a staff of approximately 8 trained sales people, and 30 to 40 production crew at any given time through those years. We were trying to teach them an understanding that they were all on the same team, and that together if they can embrace the idea of always working for efficiency we can beat not only our competition similar to our own product, but we would build such a reputation of happy customers that we would start a fever of interest in our products and services across the board to compete at a much broader level.

So my partners and I developed these *'Team Coordination and Learning Drills'* to have the entire company partake in during general staff meetings. They started with simple, and gradually moved to more and more complex. All of them were quite fun, and it seemed to crack through that barrier of understanding that each individual had on the subject of teamwork, and raise their awareness on what it truthfully was. Here is the list of drills we created, and how they worked:

Pass the Book: This was a simple one on the surface, but was a wonderful educational tool on understanding coordination. We would divide the group into two pools of 15-20 people each, and have them stand outside in the parking lot in two lines. These were the two teams competing against each other. Each would stand shoulder to shoulder facing, the two lines facing each other. A manager at one end would stand with a hardback book in hand and a stopwatch. The discipline was to have each line pass the book to the person next to each other as rapidly as possible, and each person had to have two hands on the book, and the person passing it had to say 'Here you are' and the receiving person 'Thank you' before the book could be released.

The idea was to have the book go all the way down the line as fast as possible, without violating the rules of 'Here you are' and 'Thank you' and each person having placed two hands on the book. When the person on the end received it, they were to hold the book over their head, turn around, and then pass it back up the line in the same fashion. The drill was a test of time, and accuracy.

The group that could do it the fastest was the winner. This drill the first time through is always interesting, and there are always mistakes. The discipline was to make it through without any mistakes, and be the faster team. If one only has a smaller group of say 10-15 people, then this drill can be done with one line, and the discipline is the beat the preceding time. One will find that this is a lot of fun, and it is also a great ice breaker for getting a new group to work together and become familiar with each other.

Deliver the Bear: This one is similar to the 'pass the book drill' above, but with a few differences. The teams are lined up as before, but with one major difference. They all stand shoulder to shoulder in a line, but every other person is facing the opposite direction. Also, instead of a book, a stuffed bear (preferably a very large one) is used. The same 'Here you are' and 'Thank you' rules apply, but one must now deal with the turning of the shoulders in an opposite direction to pass the bear, and each team member must have two hands on the bear before and say 'Thank you' before it can be released.

This is done timed in the same fashion as the other drill, and can be run over and over again to improve time. It adds a new level of coordination, and if anyone drops the bear the person at the front of the line must run and pick it up and run back to the start of the line and start over. The drill is timed as before with the manager at the front handing off the bear, ball or other object and using a stop watch. Run the drill over and over until everyone is feeling good that they can accomplish it. One can also increase the difficulty on this by using a large beach ball, or some other challenging object to pass (use your imagination).

Over and Under: This drill is a new level of discipline. It requires lining up as in the other two drills, but each line is facing forward, single file. Instead of being close together like the above shoulder to shoulder drills, they are all an arm's length separated from the person in front of them. A medium to large sized beach ball is used in this drill.

The person at the front of the line receives the ball at the start of the drill from the manager who hands it off and starts the clock. The first person passes it over their head to the person behind them saying 'Here you are', and the next person receives the ball with a 'Thank you' and then passes it between their legs to the person behind them, who in turn receives it in the same fashion and hands it over their head to the person behind them, and so forth.

The ball is passed over and under down the line, and the person at the end does a complete turnaround with the ball over their head and then passes it back up the line and it is returned over and under back to the start of the line and handed to the manager. This is a higher level of coordination, and once again if anyone drops the ball they must deliver it to front of the line and the drill starts over, etc.

One can also run this one with the ball being passed down the line over everyone's head, hand to hand, and then at the end the last person in line passes it back between the legs to the person behind them, and it passes all the way back up the line under in the same fashion.

Deliver the message: This is a drill designed to challenge duplication of a communication through a group of people. It is a new and different level of challenge, as it deals with simply spoken communication. One can do this with one group of people, preferably sitting in a semi-circle either on the floor or at a large conference table. Everyone sits shoulder to shoulder.

A manager writes down a simple one sentence message on a piece of paper such as *"The woods are dark at night"* or *"The moon is made of egg salad pasta"*. Something uncommonly said in everyday speech, and with a little humor mixed in helps. He or she shows the piece of paper to the first person in the semi-circle and asks them to read it silently to themselves, and memorize it without letting it be seen by anyone else in the group.

They are then instructed to whisper the message into the ear of the person next to them, but only one time. The person who receives the message must then repeat it to the person next to them, and so forth down the line until it arrives at the last person on the other side of the semi-circle.

Then this final person in the line must write down on a piece of paper what the message is and hand it to the manager who started the drill. The discipline in this drill is the teach the delivery of clearly understood communication as a point of coordination, but it also teaches the group the lesson of how communication can get distorted and altered as it passes from person to person.

For sales people to understand this is important.

Quite often they get into the belief that they can pitch their product to one spouse, and have that spouse go home and repeat the pitch to the other one successfully without the sales person being there, and have the sale occur. One learns from this that the likeliness of this being successful is greatly reduced.

This drill also teaches the discipline of making sure they understand each other as a team, especially when communicating between each other as a group. Quite often the first few times, especially with large groups, the message is extremely altered when it arrives at the end. I have found the odds are about 1 out of 10 times of it being successful on the first time through.

This one is a lot of fun and stresses the valuable lessons on many levels: Teamwork, basics of communication, clarity of the message one delivers, accuracy of message delivery, understanding each other, etc.

Name Recognition: This is another group drill that is a lot of fun. It works particularly well with teaching sales people the discipline of remembering names. This one works best with a group of 20-30 people minimum.

The team is gathered together in a room, and

each given a slip of paper which contains a name. These names can be silly or common, or more difficult as one repeats the drill. They are to read and memorize the name given to them. Once everyone has looked at their name, then they are all asked to stand up and greet 5 to 10 people each in the room (the sales manager should choose a number for each time the drill is run, progressing in difficulty) and introduce themselves, and remember the other person's name.

Once everyone has done that, then they all sit back down and are either given a sheet of paper to write down the names of the people they just met, or better yet asked individually as they go around the room to and name correctly the names of the 5 -10 people they just met. This is a test of recall, and can be expanded in difficulty to include a name and an occupation on each slip of paper.

So it runs something like this: "*Hello, my name is Peter Rabbit and I am an Organic Vegetable Specialist*" followed by "*Pleased to meet you, my name is Solomon Grundy and I am a soap and laundry detergent analyst*", etc. This drill should progress in difficultly from silly, easy to remember names, to a mix of common names like 'Smith; and 'Jones' to more complex names one can pull from a common phone book. What one is looking for as a developed discipline is for sales people to capture someone's name and occupation upon first greeting, and remember it so as to avoid asking the customer later *"What did you say your name was?"*

Whenever you can build a team that can learn this skill, the customer will feel more important and have more affinity for the sales person for them having remembered who they are and what they did. It is a great drill, and one that can be done at sales meetings as often as one wants to, and the difficulty can be increased as one chooses.

One can also substitute customer names for product names and their parts to teach the names of these items to a new group of salespeople if one chooses. The basic skill here is a test and challenge of recall, and the more one practices it, the better they can become at it.

There can be many variations on any of the above drills to adapt them to your unique business, or situation. The result of doing team drills is that is brings people together and helps to develop their skills as a group. It teaches them to coordinate together, and gives them a physical universe example of what happens when they do not coordinate properly as well.

In any of the coordination drills, I quite often would run them through it a few times, and then tell them the following: "*Okay, we are going to run this one more time, but this time I want each of you individually to work out the best position to adjust yourself to in order to maximize speed and efficiency for your part in the line.*" Once they all agreed they were ready, we would run the drill again.

These exercises help deliver home the understanding of '*competition*' and the spirit of 'contest' and at the same time build upon the foundation of doing it with a coordinated effort together, rather than as individuals. They make for a fun way to take that step forward into the realm of building teamwork with any group.

They are especially fantastic in breaking the ice with people who have never met or worked together before. It is also a great way as a manager to get the new person involved with hands-on interaction with the rest of the group, and be accepted as a teammate through the magic of personal familiarity that these drills ultimately create. So the development of teamwork is much easier to build upon after one begins with some creative exercises such as these.

Use your creativity to build upon these or invent your own, and always keep it in the direction of building upon basic skills and teach the importance of team work and you will find your other lessons you want to impart in training practices are much easier and faster, as they will start seeking help and advice from each other as well. Then the job of the sales manager becomes keeping the team heading towards a common series of goals, and achieving them, which is the ultimate unified direction one is trying to accomplish.

Open Communication

What is *open communication* as opposed to *closed communication*? Why do you as a sales manager care about these differences, and how do they apply to your role as a goal maker, and the arrival at said goals?

One could define an open communication line as a flow of information that goes both ways. It comes from a source, and arrives at a recipient. The recipient then may also originate a communication, and thus become the source.

The concept of an open communication in regards to the role of a sales manager is to keep the sales people informed of what it going in the company, as well as the industry. The return open communication makes the sales people also the eyes and ears of what is happening in the industry from the people they interact with each day, along with the things they experience. The information flows both ways, and both are invaluable.

Due to the value of this information, the communication needs to be open both ways between the sales manager and his or her sales people, and vice versa. To limit communication would be said to invite a closed communication. In some cases, on certain subjects this is necessary. However, if one likens communication to a river, and regards much like the flow of water, one can see that there is more action in a moving current than one that is dammed up. A closed communication flow could be likened in this example to a dammed up river.

What is the benefit of a flowing river of communication? Like any natural river in the world, it becomes a means of transporting information. Ships carrying cargo up and down the great Mississippi river for example also carry communication. Ferries and ships carry with them news of what I happening up river, to a greater or lesser degree. For the sales manager the vehicles of communication are their sales people. They not only need to know what is going on, they also need to know they can share communication learned and it will be accepted and utilized.

This cooperative effort on both the sales manager and the salespeople working together to keep the communication lines open is what helps to maintain a harmonious balance in the environment. With open communication, one can achieve temperance and moderation in the handling of information. It builds relationships between the sales manager and his or her team.

By having a policy of open communication between the sales manager and his or her team, both sides can experience peace of mind in the day to day goings on in the workplace. There is no barrier in place that can interrupt the flow as long as both sides agree to keep it open. In doing so, both sides can have confidence they are all heading in the same direction. The end result of such an arrangement is the forward progress towards the group goal.

With open communication, team members become players, and goals can get adjusted to avoid obstacles or becoming obsolete. Sometimes new discoveries are made that make one goal no longer valid, but with quick thinking and action it can be changed to one that is. A goal maker can make these changes only with the advantages of having an open communication with the team he or she is leading.

Some of the best things that can come from open communication are the free flowing of ideas. In my first book on this subject: *The Art of Sales Management: Lessons Learned on the Fly*, I cover the free flowing of ideas that occurs in a well run sales meeting. There are also many other ways to have open communication occurring.

One such way is to have a suggestion box where customers can contribute ideas as well. This suggestion box idea is more than just a box sitting lonely on a counter waiting for customers to take the time to write a note on a piece of paper and place it inside. No, it is much, much more. It is the invitation to respond to surveys too. This can be in the company newsletter, emails, letters, or even upon final delivery of the product. Companies that open the information door through an open communication line with their customers find out ways to improve service, and ways to improve the final product.

One can also survey the customer when they are in your place of business. Survey them at time of sale too. Ask those questions such as *'How did you find our store'* or *'What made you decide to come in today?'* I once did this as a sales manager for three months, having all the sales staff survey the customers what brought them into the store. We learned some valuable information.

One of the things we learned was the constant similar response from customers that went something like: "*I have been driving by for years and have seen your store and decided I wanted to finally stop in.*"

We later used this in our radio marketing, as it seemed from surveys that this was the constant thought from people who were driving by for years, and never coming in.

So we added the closing line of "*You have been driving by for years, don't you think it is time you stopped in?*" to all of our radio spots.

Do you know what happened as a result? Our walk-in traffic into the showroom jumped 25% over the next three months! Sales increased for the company by as much as 20%! This became a kind of subliminal advertising as we found out from our customers exactingly what they were thinking sitting in that river of cars in traffic outside our store.

There were many people who came in who heard the radio ad right when they were parked in traffic in front of the store, and turned right into our parking lot.

In fact we kept the radio station playing in the showroom, and whenever we heard the ad played it became a game to look outside in the parking lot to see who pulled in.

The benefits of keeping an open communication practice within ones business activities are many. The above is just one example. It is important to keep communication open between the sales manager and the sales team, and the team and the sales manager.

It is important also to keep the communication open between the customer and the business, and the business and the customer. One can do this by simply talking to the customer, and asking them for the information and they will tell you.

The same goes for the people you work with, and all the other communication lines one has in the running of any business, from the customer to the supplier. The better the communication flows, the stronger the growth and expansion will be.

Limiting the Limitations

No longer does a manager need to assume the notion that those working for them are limited by their existing abilities, and that hiring people is a roll of the dice in hopes that one finds that special producer who then fits into the framework of his or her team.

Over the years I have read many sales management blogs that indicate to a would-be sales manager that their role is more of a personnel hiring role, and that the success of a sales manager is in hiring people that will produce quickly.

How do you find talent?

Certainly, everyone loves to hire a new salesperson and see the enthusiasm they embrace and follow it up with that achievement of supernatural success. However, I have found this kind of profile is few and far between. To try to channel all of your success into hiring top producers only is a sure fire way to overlook real future talent. Talent is often just waiting to be discovered.

Talent is not defined by whether they can sell immediately. Few salespeople new to the profession can do this. Many seasons ones struggle, and move from sales job to sales job simply because they never were trained or helped by a sales manager over the years. Sales can be a lonely profession. It is even lonelier if one works for companies that believe people are limited, and cannot change, and therefore offer no instruction or guidance to improve them or simply *find out why they are not producing.*

With every new company anyone enters in sales, they have to learn the nuances of the product, the pricing structure, and get a feel for the product. To hire and simply throw them into an office without any support or training on these things, and then condemn them for not producing is completely irresponsible. It is also wrong for upper management to instruct the sales manager to operate this way, and then condemn them for it when this system fails.

Sales Management is about people. One must know how to inspire people, coach people and yes, take the time to *train people* even on things you consider so commonplace. New salespeople and seasoned salespeople alike need training, especially when they are new to your team. To create an environment where people are afraid to ask questions because they will feel they are presenting themselves as inadequate for the job is the wrong direction.

Sales management is about caring what is going on around you, and caring for people. It is about caring that they are successful, and have a good grounding on what the product is, how it is priced, what the services are, and how to sell it.

I have worked for companies where their whole 'training program' consisted of: *"Here is your office, here is a price list, company policy manual, and here is how you get prospects... good luck"*.

This kind of system has a high attrition rate, and it kills the spirit of good people who could become great salespeople. Sure, some will survive under this system, and many do. However, why waste so many that could become great salespeople too with a little more help?

A better system is an apprenticeship system where you not only go over the product with them; you have them sit in on the sales pitch of *other sales producers* while they are on the phone with customers. Have them listen in on *live sessions* with clients and other salespeople if such a listen-in system is available, so they can learn from watching others. Give them one-on-one instruction, and make sure they have an open communication to you as a sales manager for getting questions answered. If you can start new people with guidance, then you will see a higher rate of success.

Also, it is important to foster a *'help each other'* attitude within a company. New people should be able to go ask other more seasoned salespeople for help, without feeling they are bothering them. Treating new people like a nuisance is the way you lose them. No one wants to be treated that way. Answer their questions, and make sure others do the same in your absence. Give them a pool of information they can draw from, and you will see them grow into stable salespeople.

I liken this concept to the growing of plants in a greenhouse. If you treat the seedlings rough in the early stages, and jerk them around, don't give them water, and essentially no love, few make it. The ones that do grow seem stunted. If you take care of them, do not handle them rough, water them and talk them with words of encouragement and kindness, they grow big and strong and eventually require very little attention or care.

The same philosophy I have found true with salespeople. They need personalized attention when they are starting out along with regular words of encouragement so they feel safe and then they can get a few sales accomplished. Give them time with a few more sales, their roots will grow and they then become even more certain and confident with themselves. Eventually nothing holds them back and they can grow into as big a salesperson as their ambition leads them.

This does not mean you cannot bring in sales trainers on *techniques*, or that you as a sales manager need to be versed all the techniques. You do need to care about getting the person to have some successes, which is your primary goal. If you can do this, they can have more successes, and eventually it will build upon itself and they will be okay. Without any successes, a new salesperson can kind of go into a tail spin and it only gets worse.

So one should no longer buy into the idea that hiring is exclusively where the crux of the problem lies.

The *art of sales management* includes realizing the *potential* in people, and learning how to bring out those potentials. As a sales manager, you are limiting yourself if you believe in the idea that people are a non-changeable commodity that you can acquire, and then plug into a role and see them perform.

People have to be trained, and drilled, and even sorted out on *their own goals* as well in order to make them produce. Somewhere along the line, every successful salesperson you hire had someone who helped them to a greater or lesser degree in this area before they came to you. So dispossess yourself of the idea that people cannot change, improve or achieve greatness just because they do not show it on day one, week one or even month one.

Learn the balance between apprenticing people, and letting go of the reigns once they are taking off with the role. The basic core of an individual is that they do want to succeed, and most are trying when they take on a new job.

Look for the overwhelmed person, and help them become less overwhelmed by breaking down what they are struggling with to simpler steps. Go back to their basics, and basic material about the product they are selling, and make sure there is nothing that they did not understand and help them sort it out. Not every product is easy to understand, so help them understand it by going back over it step by step if needed.

What should a hiring department focus on?

Certainly a human resources department should be screening a person out for basic skills such as *being able to read*, *write* and do *basic math*. Also grammar can be a quality in certain fields as well. Once the candidate becomes a member of your team, one should be able to sort out anyone if they have these basic skills. However, if this becomes a problem, and the hiring department does not have a high enough bar for pre-qualifications, you as a sales manager can certainly make sure they raise that bar.

As an example, I once added into the application and testing process the requirement that the applicant write a short essay of at least 3 paragraphs on *why they wanted to work for our company, and how they can help people by doing this*.

The essay taught me many things. It gave me an idea how they communicated. It gave me an understanding of their grammar level, their ability to communicate ideas, and also spelling. By having the question about helping people, it gave me an idea on their intentions as well, and whether they had a grasp on helping clients, or realized the connection with clients, colleagues, and their company, besides themselves. It is hard to read too much into an essay, but it is a good way to at least see a few additional things that won't come out in a basic general application or test.

You can also make this essay requirement a little longer if you wish, and have them write three of them. Here are some good questions you might want to ask them to write about:

- *How could your working for this company help others? Who would those people be?*

- *What would you consider to be a great day in sales if you were to be hired as a salesperson for our team?*

- *What does teamwork mean, and what does it have to do with you?*

Do not worry about taking too much of an applicant's time in the hiring process. If they really want the job they will comply with any number of steps you require in the applications. Do not concern yourself with this. In fact, if they get impatient, this too can be an indicator or part of the test. Patience is something you cannot test for easily, but it certainly makes a huge difference with working with customers. An impatient person on a sales team can drive away customers.

Having some information on how they think and what their ideas are tends to come out in the essays. The next step is a personal interview, after you read their application and essays. What you are trying to find out in the interview is their composure, self confidence, and work ethics among other things.

As a sales manager, I would let personnel do their initial screening interviews for the company, and then if they were approved after that, I would interview them myself to find out more about them personally. I did not concern myself so much with if they could produce, but whether they were willing to learn. If they had an attitude of 'I know all about it' and could not demonstrate a production record, this was a red flag for me.

There is nothing wrong with confidence, if one can back it up with evidence. However, anyone who seemed head-strong that they 'knew everything there was to know about sales' in the interview I would then proceed with caution as to whether I would hire them. I would give them a grace period if I hired them, telling it was a trial period, and if they could do as they say, we would hire them on full time. Too often I learned that charlatans would apply for the position, and had no real production record, and because they had the wrong attitude that *they knew everything already*, you could not teach them anything new or correct them easily. I preferred to hire people new or experienced who had the attitude that there is always something new to learn about anything, and one can always improve.

So if you want to add quality people to your team to better achieve your goals, then have a good screening process to begin with that covers important skills and then a good follow up plan to train and apprentice them. This is the way you remove all limitations and rocket together towards goals by always harvesting tomorrow's crop of new and experienced salespeople alike. In this way one can limit ones idea on the limitations of others, and get on with the business and success of being a goal maker.

Breaking down what is Important

Whenever one is leading others, one must be able to isolate what is important from what is not. What is vital and necessary, and what is supernumerary. When one can do this, one can make decisions based on logic, and not on impulse. What is the most essential importance's around you that are necessary to survival? As opposed to the ones you would like to have, but are not essential to immediate survival?

Let's say one is faced with a decision where a

sales person comes to you asking for the afternoon off to go resolve a personal problem with their spouse. Let's say you as a manager are short handed and really cannot see logically giving the person the extra time off.

In this situation one must look at the problem from two opposing points of view at least. One, you are short handed and need all of your sales people scheduled on duty. Two, if you leave this person on the floor with an unresolved problem with their spouse, is their head really going to be involved fully in the task at hand?

One response says he or she should stay and finish their shift, and deal with their personal problems later. The other clearly says to let them go, as they will be of no use to the group with this unresolved problem.

The decision in such a case is not a matter of right or wrong, but a matter of Importance's. Which is of the greater importance? The sales manager will perhaps have to dig further into the personal situation to gain this knowledge. One can also empower the other salesperson to solve it for themselves by calling another fellow salesperson to come in and cover for them, or agreeing to work extra hours later in the week, or some combination, etc.

So in a situation such as this there are many

importance's to factor in. The obvious importance: to the individual, also to the other members of the team, the customers, etc. So isolating what is the most important becomes the root of making a decision on any decision, be is a small situation as defined here, or a large one that one may later face.

At the extreme in such a situation, a sales manager must also recognize that a member on their team with too many life distractions can become a liability. Perhaps in a scenario like that granting the person a leave of absence to go off to resolve their issues before returning might be a better solution. No one wants to lose good people, but if they do not have their head in the game it can disrupt the harmony of those they work around.

In another scenario, let's look at a situation where you have a group of sales people, and some are really turning in the numbers and a few are just riding the clock. Let's say that one that is really producing approaches you as a sales manager asking for an unscheduled day off. Let assume a short while later one of the clock riding sales people on your team approached you with a similar request for the same day off. How do you break down the importance in this situation? One could struggle with 'equal opportunity' viewpoint or the viewpoint rewarding your most productive worker. I always favored rewarding the most productive, and found that to be the most successful in terms determining what is important.

These sorts of situations all come down to decisions by a sales manager, and learning how to make them and at the same time achieve the goals of the group. What decision will make for the higher likelihood of your group meeting the goals? Happy and satisfied productive salespeople therefore become an integral part of that goal. Rewarding those that do not produce would work the opposite and perhaps make it so the group mirrors the actions of the one who is lazy, rather than follow in the footsteps of those that take their job seriously and work at it.

So when trying to sort out what is the right decision and what is important, one should probably filter those decisions through the following questions for best results:

- *What decision will help the group best achieve its goals?*

- *Which decision will increase productivity?*

Certainly a sales manager could be tempted into thinking with just his sales quota, and let the non-producer take the day off in favor of having his or her best salesperson stay on duty. This on the surface might sound like a solid logical economic decision. However, how would the high producer feel? Is not a day off a reward? Has he or she that is a top producer entitled to more latitude in their requests for an extra day off? Also, if one gives the one who is lazy an extra day off, simply because one would rather not have them around, what does that say about you as a manager? Are you not also sending a message to others about how you care?

There is nothing more cancerous to the morale of a group than an "I don't care attitude" from someone at the top. It spreads like the Exxon Valdez oil spill across the morale of the group, and it is difficult if not impossible to turn around after it has spread too far. Professional sports teams will experience this at times, and they will go through an entire overhaul of the roster from top management on down to turn the franchise back in a positive direction again.

Witness the Detroit Lions team of 2008 when they became the first team ever to go 0-16 on the season. In 2009 they had a new general manager, head coach, and had cut almost half the players on the roster. It took years for them to shed that stigma, and be considered a contender again.

So as a sales manager, there becomes a background pattern of 'What is of senior importance in this matter before me' that underscores the ultimate decision process.

Sometimes the importance is not the one on the surface that is obvious. Therefore further personal inquiries become necessary when making determinations between individuals as given in the above examples to make an effective decision.

We can also establish the facts that there are different levels of what is important. There are matters of senior importance, and there are matters of junior importance. These are easy to distinguish in juxtaposition. However, it is the third area of importance that lays the most difficult challenge. That is the gray area in between, and this is where the sales manager must be able to make the right decision. Even if he or she is just 51% right, it is important to attempt to be on the side of 51% rather than the 49% in those decisions that are very close to call.

Following Through

When someone is able to achieve their goals as an individual they do so through the use of creative abilities and skill and using the tools available to them. With a group, it is the creative skills of a collective of individuals that makes it possible for the group to achieve the group goal.

When one begins in the direction in pursuit of a goal for a group, it is usually a goal set by a goal maker. In order to follow through with the completion of that goal, the individuals in the group must not only use their creative skill, talents and resourcefulness to make it a reality, they must first launch the endeavor with inspiration.

To embark in the direction of a goal set by a goal maker, individuals must believe it is possible to achieve. They must also embrace the ideal achieving that goal embodies. In the birth of any new idea or project, there is always the need to focus energy to the task at hand. Such energy comes in many forms. It can be in terms of individual effort, time committed and even financial resources.

It is difficult to take on a large goal all by oneself. In some cases it can be done. With groups, it requires the commitment from all involved. There has to be a unified agreement to follow through, and work day in and day out to make that goal a reality. Most large goals cannot be accomplished in a day. They require weeks, months and sometimes years achieving. To span that time the individuals must not only be committed to the goal, but also be committed to following through.

When we talk about following through, we are talking about persistence in the daily adventure of moving forward towards the accomplishment of the endeavor wherein at some point the end result will be achieved.

For example, it takes quite a bit of persistence as

an individual to hike the entirely of the Appalachian trail in the Eastern U.S. The trail is over 2100 miles long. Each year, thousands of hikers embark on the trail in an attempt to hike it all the way through (called a 'Thru-hike) and only one in four achieve their goal. There is essentially two parts to any long term success in following a long term goal.

> 1. *Belief in the goal itself, and having a personal and group commitment to obtaining it.*
>
> 2. *Being committed to the follow through.*

The 'Follow Through' is the daily grind of what it takes to accomplish the next step on the journey, despite all the day to day opposition from life itself. This opposition comes in many, many forms. All of these can knock someone sideways off the railroad tracks as they attempt to follow through, and one must be able to observe this opposition for what it is and continue to follow through.

Here is a list of some of the common manifestations of 'opposition' that one faces when trying to accomplish a goal, and which if allowed to overtake the efforts will derail an individual or group from accomplishing its end goals:

I. An outside force trying to harness the energy of the follow though and commitment, and change its direction for the short term or even long term.

II. An injected plan into the works to make one step of the journey more complicated than it needs to be.

III. An arbitrary introduction of new 'standards' that must be met to accomplish the goal, and thus making the entire endeavor financially impossible to achieve.

IV. The removal of key personnel from outside forces, thus wiping out those with the crucial energy to carry the project through to completion.

V. The introduction of insane ideas into the mixture of an otherwise sane path to the goal, causing the group to wander off the path.

VI. Individuals within the group creating self generated negative publicity or propaganda about the project, and thus killing the spirit of the activity through public opinion and negative reports.

VII. The efforts of one individual or a small few obsessed with control and power, denying the participation and contribution of all the members of the group, thus causing the group to collapse.

VIII. Engaging in illegal or corrupt activities.

IX. Failing to remind the group members daily, weekly and monthly of the goal and charting its progress for all to see.

X. Individuals within the group who are not committed to the goal will sometimes be covertly withholding this from the other members of the group, while at the same time trying to destroy the efforts of the group from accomplishing smaller steps along the way.

These are just ten examples. There can be many, many more. All efforts are counter to the efforts of following through on the path to accomplishing the goal. In order to overcome these efforts to derail the group from achieving the end goal, and following through, one must be able to recognize these actions when they occur. The solution is not to combat it head on, but to overwhelm the counter energy with positive energy and despite all odds pushing forward with success.

Sometimes outside forces can become overpowering and may even remove or destroy the goal maker in an effort to stop the goal from being achieved, or divert the energy to a new direction to suit their own goals. Members of the group need to recognize that this can occur as well, and offer support and protection for the goal maker.

However, this is not always possible, and thus even a goal maker must be able to see when the efforts and follow through needed to accomplish a goal far outweigh the end value of reaching the goal. At that point, they must either abandon that goal for a new one, or abandon the group and seek to accomplish the goal from a different direction where the counter energy cannot stop them.

When one embarks on a goal that is worthwhile, one never expects to run into opposition merely because the end goal is so valuable and beneficial. However, it is a fact that in our world there are people who do not want things improved or bettered. There are people who exist only to alter, divert or destroy efforts of others to accomplish positive goals. This is especially true when it comes to accomplishing goals that will result in helping others once completed.

These people live in fear of other people being successful, and thus will invent all manner of smoke and mirrors in an effort to stop ones ambition to follow through and complete a goal.

In unfavorable situations, negative elements throw obstacles in the way of the progress towards a goal, such as pessimism, or injecting a lack of realism upon the group or simply themselves having the overwhelming inability to accept a helping hand, thus opening the door for failure.

Sometimes these negative elements can be neutralized, and one can carry on. Other times these forces bring to a screeching halt any forward progress. Like a locomotive with its engine destroyed and fused to the tracks, it will take too much energy to get it moving again, and one might make better progress by taking a footpath in a new direction without all the burdens it carries with it.

As a sales manager or a manger of any kind, one must learn the skill of being able to choose their battles, and which ones are worth fighting for. Thus parallel to the skill of being able to follow through to accomplish a goal is the ability to recognize when it is time to abandon one where too much of the hillside is already ablaze with counter efforts and counter energy.

Life goes on, and there is always another day. Sometimes it is best to just grab your knapsack, and strap on some hiking boots, and take the footpath in a new direction even if it means starting over. Following through can mean many things at many levels. One must never lose sight of following through on their own goals as well, and when they are so far out of alignment with the group goals, it is the wise man or woman who can recognize that and move on.

Harmony

When discussing the subject of harmony can best be described as: 'A consistent, orderly, or pleasing arrangement of parts' and sometimes it is defined as 'Congruity' or 'Agreement in feeling, actions, ideas, interest or opinion'. It also is defined by Webster's Dictionary as 'Peaceable or friendly relations.'

So at the root is the concept of 'agreement' and 'peaceful relations' which are ultimately brought about by agreements within a group or activity. If one has agreement with all involved, then one can easily have harmony as all the players can work together on a common cause. In order to maintain a constant level of success as a sales manager, one needs to achieve a level or harmony within the team.

In Chinese Philosophy, the concept Yin - Yang (also called Yin and Yang) is a belief that seemingly opposing or contrary forces are placed together in harmony despite their differences. The concept embraces the idea that these opposing forces are interconnected and yet interdependent; much like night and day, or shadow and sunlight.

The philosophy of Taoism discusses these natural opposites or 'dualities' such as hot and cold, low and high, water and fire, life and death, masculine and feminine, and so on. They are symbolized by a circle divided into two separate parts gracefully by a curved line, and one half black and the other white. However, each has a circle of the other inside their respective halves. This symbol portrays the balance of nature, and life itself, and at the same time making each a co-existent part of the other.

Yin is often referred to as the passive or feminine force in the universe. Yang is the active or masculine force in the universe. If one is facing a problem that lacks harmony, can you not examine it as a sales manager and determine if a passive response will bring about harmony, or an active response will do so?

In a position of a sales manager, one can take this ancient concept and apply it to the team to understand harmony and balance. One can divide the activity of sales into several dualities in its many aspects, and by considering these separate parts can unite these dualities and create harmony. One could say that there are many dualities that exist in sales, and together they create a unified whole of that aspect of the subject.

Here are some examples:

Training - Practical use

Speaking - Listening

Customer - No Customer

Communicating - Silence

Hidden - Revealed

Known - Unknown

Question - Answer

Rest - Activity

Contraction - Expansion

If you take some time and examine your sales

area, you could quite easily come up with many others that when combined create harmony.

Let's take 'training' for example. Training only serves as half of the activity; no matter how hard you train it does not become complete for you as an individual until you stop training, and apply it in real life with a customer. Only then can you use both training and practical application to create a sale, and thus a whole.

If one only speaks to the customer, and never listens, one will only be existing in one half of the actual process. Only when one balances both speaking and listening does one have a complete understanding of the needs of that customer, and thus place one in a position to create the sale.

Then there is the broader duality of having a customer and not having a customer. One has a customer, and loses another. Only when one understands what made the customer you have arrive, and the one that was lost 'go' that one can have a harmony of understanding about the comings and goings of customers.

If one focuses strictly on the customer one gained, and ignores the one that was lost, that lack of understanding on the one that was lost will create further losses. Likewise, if one spends all their energy on trying to salvage the ones that were lost, and ignores the ones that are present, one will lose the incoming ones as well. Thus having knowledge of both of these creates a unified understanding.

Additionally there are communications the customer is willing to give, and ones they answer only with silence. This become also information revealed, and information they are hiding. If one does not seek to understand both, one will not find they are arriving at a sale. A sales manager trains his or her people to not only find out what they customer is saying, but also to discover what they are not saying so that they can remain in control of the sales process.

Further one can discover that rest is important and in balance with action. Working too long without sleep will make one ineffective, and likewise sleeping too ling without action can make one lazy and also ineffective. A balance of both is required for longevity.

As a sales manager, one must also realize the relationship between contraction and expansion. One can expand, and at the same time the duality of the universe will cause an equal amount of contraction.

So one must learn this balance, and understand these differences to be able to make an area grow. A company can grow for quite awhile in one direction, and become the juggernaut of their times, but eventually they begin contracting as the industry is replaced by newer technologies, newer people, or the founder with the driving force retires, etc. History is filled with companies that were once the dominant force in their day, like: E.F. Hutton, TWA, Woolworth's and General Foods that no longer exist. So one can seek to expand, but one must also be aware that there may come a time when contraction follows.

When one is discussing harmony in a group of sales people, the balance must also embrace fairness and honesty. Giving an equal footing to every sales person on the team, with the options to use those resources and grow is what helps to create harmony. Playing favoritism to one, and not the others will create disharmony. To be successful in managing any group, one must create an environment of fairness. One cannot upbraid one salesperson for a particular mistake, and fail to do the same with the next one, for example.

One must also create an environment where the structure is in harmony as well. Creating equal time on shifts, and equal access to customers can sometimes be difficult, but it is the task of the sales manager to attempt to do this.

Whenever one is facing a difficult situation or incident under ones charge, it is helpful to know this rule of Yin and Yang, and be able to examine the situation from that perspective. Is there something that is missing in this scenario?

If things are too clouded and heavy, would it not be good as a sales manager to introduce some sunshine and open blue skies to the event at hand?

If there is a problem with customers are leaving because your competition is offering better service, does it make sense for you to stay with just what you have always done? Would it not be better to examine the duality of the Yin and Yang on this situation, and introduce the opposite of what you have always done, and perhaps offer better service to the customers?

Certainly every situation will be unique, but as a sales manager one must look at this basic law as it relates to harmony, and consider it. A very simple approach to resolving this is if you see something that is disharmony, ask yourself after you look closely at it: 'what is missing?'

Sometimes stepping in and taking an active role in handling the situation is needed directly by the sale manager first hand. Other times, a presence, but one with a more passive role is what is needed to bring about harmony with the customer. There is a balance that one comes to understand and apply with this, and it too requires practice.

Honesty & Trust

Honest is said to be the quality of living with the truth. Trust is defined as "A firm belief in the reliability, truth, ability, or strength of someone or something." As a sales manager one must personify trust among those he or she seeks to lead. There can be no divergence from this rule. The moment you do something that is deemed untrustworthy by a salesperson you are managing, it is an uphill battle to ever regain that trust again 100%. There will always be a watchful eye on what you do, and a doubt about your sincerity in which you do something.

Honesty and trust are built upon ones willingness to assume the responsibility of the position in which you are occupying. Are you doing the job simply because it is a paycheck? Or do you believe in the long terms goals that you set, or the ones set by your company? Sales management success hinges on your ability to embrace the goals you set, and take responsibility for the outcome, good or bad. In this way you build upon the foundation of trust.

HONESTY REQUIRES COURAGE

It takes courage to admit when you make a mistake or were wrong. It takes honesty to clear the air on it with the individuals involved, and get things back on track. Mistakes happen. Bad decisions are made that can place one on the wrong path at times. Every manager in any capacity will face this at time. No one is perfect. However, one needs to have the personal responsibility level within oneself that guides them to own up for the error in judgment and correct it, and move on. If you can do this, you will gain respect from those you lead.

There is no dishonor in making a mistake. There is dishonor in discovering the mistake and continuing to inflict it upon the group because you cannot take the responsibility for having put it there in the first place. So in the process of being willing to try new things, one must be mindful and observant that when an error in judgment is made that one needs to correct it quickly.

The wrong personnel on a post can destroy the group, for example. I once had a receptionist that was hired. She turned out to be illiterate. I had her work on a project for me of organizing the phone numbers of contractors and clients. She misspelled all the names, and effectively scrambled the records. It took me months to sort out after I let her go. It was a mistake not to require a literacy test. This was corrected, and the next person hired was more competent. It was a lesson in responsibility as a manager to discover the mistake, and correct it rapidly. To not do so would have created further problems with the group, as she would have mixed up other files, and client records and created havoc if she had been given more jobs to do that were similar.

I have known businesses to hire someone, and retain them just because the owner who hired them could not confront that they made an error in hiring the person. They had entrusted the individual with so much responsibility, and even paid money for special training only to learn they were ineffective and abusive to other employees and even customers. To hold onto such a mistake will wear on the confidence of others that work for you, and lower their trust in your judgment.

So there is a lot to be said on the subject of using judgment, but more importantly the value of being able to take responsibility for one's own actions, even in the position of a manager. If you ignore a problem, it will come back to bite you. It will also cost more money in the long run.

Therefore one learns a thing or two about honest, trust and responsibility as a manager:

- *Be responsible in the decisions you make.*

- *Be responsible enough to recognize a mistake when made.*

- *Take action without waiting if it bears out as a mistake.*

- *Confront the problem immediately, and resolve it quickly.*

- *Hide nothing from those you lead who were affected by the error, and clear the air swiftly.*

- *Build trust through effective causative actions in all that you do.*

If you can learn to do the above, you will not be fearful of making decisions as you go along. Additionally, you will not restrain yourself in taking action quickly in times when you made a poor decision. If you do, your reputation of being honest to yourself and others will build with those you lead. You will also build their trust, as they will know that you will take action on a problem to resolve it, rather than let it become an encysted infection on the life and survival of the group simply because you do not want to confront that you were wrong.

DON'T DO ANYTHING ILLEGAL

Honesty also has to do with leading a clean life. Not engaging in illegal or dishonest business practices, or doing anything that is in violation of the law. So as a sales manager no matter what product you are selling, always know and teach the legal aspects and the law related to the product you are selling. Do this even if you have to hire an attorney to clarify issues.

ACT WITH FAIRNESS, BE CONSISTENT IN JUDGMENT

When dealing with any issues between sales people you are managing, always be fair with all dealings between them. Do not grant special privileges to one, and not the other, regardless of tenure. Always make sure your decision making actions on any judgment call are consistent from situation to situation. Do not make it a penalty to don something one week, and not enforce it the next week when someone does it again. To conduct one this way build distrust, and you will lose respect in how you resolve issues. You will develop a reputation of being unfair, and this can fester into a great deal of disharmony.

BE PREDICTABLE

Part of the success of being a sales manager is becoming that stable person for the sales people to rely on. To create this as a possibility, one must be able to be predictable in all ones actions and responses. Here are some important things not to do:

- *Don't make yourself available one day, and then chase them away the next.*

- *Don't say one type of deal is okay on one day, and not the next unless you have a reason.*

- *Never favor one sales person's deals over the next.*

- *Never say you will be available or at an appointment at a specific time, and then not show.*

- *Never be firm on one issue and then weak on it the next.*

BE OF EVEN TEMPERAMENT

No one wants to talk to an angry person. No one really wants to be around a wimpy one either. As a sales manager you cannot afford the luxury of wearing your personal emotions on your sleeve. You must remain even in temperament in all your day to day actions, despite the stress of the job.

It is all too easy to get off the phone with an angry person and then blow up at the next person who walks into your office. Don't do it. Learn to harness the emotion the moment the minute the conversation ends. Take a moment of silence, or go outside for a walk around the block if you feel out of control of your emotions, but do not vent it on someone else. It never serves of any value, and makes that person who receives such a communication hesitate the next time they need to come see you.

Always remain a persona of even temperament even if you do not feel that way all the time. Find a colleague outside the office in a similar line of work to vent to if you need to do this, but make sure they are not connected to those you are managing. I would never recommend that you download on your spouse, as this never really serves to benefit your personal life in the long run.

Take that advice from a married man. It can place unnecessary strain in your personal life simply because your spouse generally does not know how to help you resolve it, especially if they are not in a managerial position themselves.

By the same token, no matter how upset you are about something, never throw anger at someone to resolve the situation. This goes especially, if they are the wrong target for this emotion. I am not saying that a person never needs a good chewing out. No, some people do, and that is the only way they will turn around. However, one needs to pause a moment before acting, rather than acting irrationally and then later regretting it.

People who continually, carelessly and maliciously create problems are the correct target usually for this kind of emotion. In those situations a good 'chewing out' benefits the group, who suffered from their negligent actions, often more than the person themselves. However, one needs to be able to do this without losing control of emotions, and being reckless about how one handles it. So one learns as a sales manager that there is a balance, but at its foundation is an even temperament.

SUPPORT

Being a person that is supportive in their moment of trouble is what a sales manager's common action is. One needs to be a never ending resource for encouragement and support, especially when a sales person is having a difficult time on the job. That backbone of support it what also helps strengthen their trust with you. You will also know as an index of how well you are doing as a sales manager if your team feels they can freely come to you with any difficulty, and does so without hesitation. Then you know also that they consider you to be not only worthy of their trust, but that you are honest in your dealings with them and the group.

Understanding Games

When we examine the subject of games, it is easy to break it down into subsections. One has players, rules, objectives, goals, competitors, equipment, rewards and often a coach. The activity of sales can be compared to a game in its day to day operations. As a sales manager, games are a useful tool to guide a group in a playful way towards the established goals.

Games can be intense. They can be exciting. They can be fun. People engaged on a competitive industry like sales enjoy games. It makes life exciting, and helps build upon teamwork.

PLAYERS

Players are those members of your team. To have 'players' on a team one must first having willingness to play. It is not so much a matter of calling out that you have a game in progress, the players themselves need to be a willing participant. One can get willingness by allowing them to participate in the creation of the game, and making it their own.

RULES

Every game needs rules, or there are likely no guidelines in which to play. Some of the basic rules of any game are the start and finish. Other rules consist of how points are scored, and what constitutes a reward and what does not. It also defines who wins, who the competition is and who gets to celebrate when the game is won.

OBJECTIVES

Just like in sports, there is an objective. In baseball it is to get around the bases and score more runs than your opponent. In American football or soccer, the objective is the get the ball into or across the goal line. In hockey it is getting the puck in the net, and in basketball it is getting the ball in the basket.

Objectives are important in lining up any game for sales people, as it gives them a goal to march towards. This is an important factor for a goal maker, as the vehicle of games helps your group arrive closer to your defined goal.

GOALS

Goals are the obtainable accomplishments one is heading towards. It is the end result. Every game should have a goal. An example of a sales goal could be a highest ever monthly sales volume for a month in the year, or the achievement of a specific sales quota or target set at the beginning.

COMPETITORS

In any game there is the competition. Who is the competition in a sales game? It could be a game between stores. It could be just the marketplace where the consumer spends their dollar. If your sales team is large enough it could be played between team 'A' and team 'B', or guys against gals, or the inside sales team versus the outside sales team, etc. Make sure you define who the competing teams are before you begin.

EQUIPMENT

Every game requires equipment. Players in

sports have things like helmets and pads, and the ball. In sales, one needs paper, computers, phones, leads, charts, etc. Find out what is needed in terms of equipment to run your game and make sure it is available. Usually any sales game among a group needs at least a common chart or scoreboard so all can monitor the progress throughout the progress of the game. Also important in any game is the score keeper. As a sales manager, you often serve as both the coach and referee.

REWARDS

What is the reward if one wins? In any game there needs to be the reward. It can be individual bonuses or recognition for the salespeople or it can be a group award. The reward must be something they will play for, or you will have no game. Surveying what they will play for is a good way to start as a sales manager. It is likely something you would never dream, and is quite often simple or doable for you to offer.

There can be some debate as to whether a cash reward is what motivates or a non-cash reward does. I have always found it is best to survey the group of people to see what motivates them. One should carefully construct the questions so as not to be leading in either way. Ask general questions of 'What type of reward would you play a sales game for?' or 'What should a salesperson receive if they make ___ goal?' You might find the results vary and are surprising depending on the group you survey. I once surveyed a group of sales people and found out that a special 'day off' was more desirable than a cash reward, as an example.

Some other examples of non-cash rewards could be a special parking space, recognition (as in a plaque), time off to be with family, a vacation, ticket to the ball game, etc.

TYPES OF GAMES THAT CAN BE PLAYED

There are many ways to execute a game or series of games for sales people to play. Some can be short term, and others ongoing. I have provided a list of some common examples here for you to consider for your sales team.

Salesperson of the 'Week', 'Month' and 'Year'

The salesperson of the week, month and year game is essentially a game that is played ongoing throughout the year. Each week a salesperson who is the highest seller for week is acknowledged and given a small reward. Each month on the first day the salesperson of the prior month is acknowledged, has their name engraved on a plaque and given various rewards and bonuses. Annually the salesperson of the year is acknowledged usually at a special company dinner, and they are feted with their family, given a plaque, and bonus.

Quota achievement games

These are generally short term games bracketed within a 1-2 week time frame usually to break a group out of a slump. A specific quota for group sales is met, a timeframe defined and a bonus is set for all to achieve. It can be a group game or an individual achievement game, or both.

Highest ever games

This is another example of an easy to administer ongoing game. This is where an established bonus is rewarded to any sales person that reaches their 'highest-ever' sales amount or number of units sold in a given week or month. Rewards are usually a monetary bonus of some kind.

Inventory sell out games

Sometimes managers need to get a group of sales people to focus and concentrate on a particular type of company inventory that needs to be sold off before a new product can be introduced. Setting up short or long term games on a particular inventory with a special cash reward bonus for selling that type of product is one way to do this. Another is to establish a group game where everyone can play to sell off this inventory and receive a group bonus for working together to accomplish this.

Highest ever number of unit sales

Sometimes sales dollar volumes are too complicated and not meaningful enough to a team of sales people to get them inspired to sell in a game environment. Thus an alternative game to be focused on 'number of units' of a particular product to make it something that is simpler and one they will play for. Car dealerships frequently play with this one, as it is easier to count number of cars and predict and control that, than a specific dollar volume at times.

Reaching a quota or highest ever of a 'special type of product' sales

Sometimes a special type of product is in season and desirable to sell before the season comes to a close. Running a game on the sale of snow mobiles in January might be a good way to clear the showroom for other summer products come April or May for example. So setting up a game with a reward system for reaching a quota of selling this special type of inventory can be a useful tool for a sales manager to utilize in boosting sales.

New territory sales

A sales manager desiring to get their product sold in a new geographic area could effectively set up a game for sales people to reward them when they sold within that area defined on a map. This works best when one has field sales people.

SUMMARY

Games are fun. Games must be fun to be played. Remember to always consult the player's willingness, and play the role universally of the supportive coach and the even handed referee and any game can become a huge success for a sales manager.

Resilience & Continuity

    In order to make goals a reality, one must develop the skills to become resilient despite all obstacles. Continuous forward progress is all one can cling to when times become challenging. Every sales manager faces difficult times and better times throughout their career. How one does one deal with it is that allows one to survive?

    Stress is a part of life in any workplace. Sales managers must deal with loss of personnel, sick personnel, mistakes by personnel, upset customers, budget cuts within the company, new regulations externally as well as industry changes on a day to day basis. It is important during this time for one to develop some skills to allow themselves to become focused.

There are six key areas that a sales manager needs to focus on personally in order to maintain resilience and continuity, and overcome stress. These are as follows:

- *Keeping oneself moving*
- *Apply good eating habits*
- *Drink alcohol only in moderation, don't take harmful drugs and limit your nicotine or stop smoking altogether*
- *Get a good night's sleep*
- *Expand one's base of knowledge*
- *Seek a spiritual outlook*

In these six key areas one can gain some relief not only of stress in the day to day operation, but also some more control in life. Part of it expands the body; the others address the mind and spirit.

KEEP ONESELF MOVING

Go to the gym. Take time each day to exercise your body, or at least walk around the city block or park. Ride a bike to work if necessary, but get your body some exercise. This will help you in the long run in terms of energy and dealing with stress. Any activity that raises your heart rate and gets you to sweat is good for the system, and will help you with relaxation. For constantly improving stress relief, try to get at least 30 minutes of heart-moving activity daily. If it's easier for you to fit into your schedule, break the activity up into two or three shorter segments if need be.

APPLY GOOD EATING HABITS

Low blood sugar can make you feel anxious and irritable, while eating too much can make you lethargic. Too much sugar can make you feel zapped of energy, and too little carbohydrates can make you hungry and irritable. Balance your intake with vitamin rich foods like vegetables, and fruit. See a nutritionist about healthy eating habits, or read books on the subject for better health. Avoid fast food and junk food. Eating right can give you the right energy level, and reduce tiredness and stress.

DRINK ALCOHOL ONLY IN MODERATION, DON'T TAKE HARMFUL DRUGS & LIMIT YOUR NICOTINE OR

STOP SMOKING ALTOGETHER

Artificial stimulants work only in the short term, and take a longer toll on the body. Over time one can become more tired; demanding more one intakes of such substances, a dependency can develop. Although sometimes these things can appear in the short term help relieve stress, in the long term they can reduce vitamin levels in the body, alter metabolism, and result in lack of sleep or proper rest.

GET A GOOD NIGHT'S SLEEP

Not only can stress and worry can cause insomnia, but a lack of sleep can leave you vulnerable to even more stress. When you're well-rested, it's much easier to keep your emotional balance, a key factor in coping with your job and the workplace related stress. Getting a good night's sleep and acquiring the ability to 'shut off' the work for the day is essential to being able to reset yourself mentally for the next day.

EXPAND ONE'S BASE OF KNOWLEDGE

Achieving resilience and continuity against all obstacles one faces through the daily and weekly actions of a sales manager requires not only addressing basic matters physically. It requires expanding ones knowledge on a continual basis as well.

Take time for yourself and study. Learn new

things. Go to the library, or read more eBooks online. Visit your local bookstore and read new books. Expand your knowledge and skill. Share these nuggets of wisdom you learn with those that you work with through sales meetings and training skills.

  The day to day actions of a sales manager can through at them a lot of different situations. Make a list of the things you have difficulty with. Keep a journal at your desk. One for successful actions and day to day operations, and one for the things that you come to realize you need to expand your knowledge in. The global internet resources available today can place knowledge and information at your fingertips in moments. Take time to gain some new knowledge each day.

  If you do this, and make it a part of your daily routine, it will likely become contagious to others around you and you can lead by example. Expanding one's knowledge on a regular basis is an integral part of being a long term successful sales manager.

SEEK A SPIRITUAL OUTLOOK

  Everyone has some kind of a belief spiritually to a greater or lesser degree. This section is not to stress a particular religious faith. The point here is that in order to stay focused, one sometimes needs to remember there is a spiritual side to life. It can be as simple as taking a moment out of your day to spend walking in the park, and looking at animals and plants. It can mean spending time playing with your children or grand children. It can also mean going to church, or praying. No matter whether you follow a religious doctrine or not, one can recognize to some degree when they are alone that there is more to life than just flesh and tissue. Seek to explore that spirituality for oneself, and disconnect for awhile from the day to day stress of operations. Take some time to yourself, and relax. Let go. You will feel better, and be able to re-enter the stressful environment with a fresh viewpoint now and again. It is always well worth it.

Vitality

Another finer point about understanding living is that one needs to have a sense of vitality. What is *'vitality'?* Vitality is defined as: *'The state of being strong and active; energy.'* It also refers to: *'The power giving continuance to life and it is considered to be present in all living things'*.

Vitality is living with a sense of energy. Do you sometimes feel a sensation that you are just lacking energy? As a sales manager, this is deadly. One has to be larger than life in guiding sales personnel. One cannot sit at a desk and push paper and hope for the best. If you are feeling a sensation of 'no energy' then you lack the 'continuance' you need to add vitality in the work place.

In plant life, vitality is considered to be the capacity for them to live, grow and endeavor. In people, the same rules apply. One needs to create one's own vitality. It is done through getting into motion. One simple way is to get in a routine of daily exercise, and another is simply making your rounds through the office. For exercise, go to the gym and work out as often as you can get there, even if it is just using the tread mill.

In the office, don't just sit and wait for life to come to you! Go out and find it! Observe your people at work at their stations. Make your rounds. Be of good cheer, and give out positive words of encouragement daily to all those that you work with. Share a funny story, or inspiring one. Make sure you communicate good news, not negativity.

Negativity should be banned from your environment. Always foster a positive environment, and you will begin to feel the daily energy and excitement of living. Make sure you impart that to your sales people as well. Encourage them to exercise, take walks and enjoy the sunshine once in awhile. Bring the sunshine to them too!

Sales can be a very rough job. One interacts with all kinds of people daily. Not all of them are friendly. Some are downright mean. This negativity can rub off on people, and make them feel grumpy or bitter. Make sure you keep the proper attitude yourself and be there to lift them up. It is the vitality of living. You must inject life into the environment, as it will not do it on its own.

There is so much negativity in the world at large. Bad news pollutes the internet, radio and television. People do not realize how this affects them. It can poison their attitude about living, and crush their spirits. As a sales manager, one needs to realize that *we create our own attitudes*. We create our own vitality.

Become the contagious vitality in your environment. Share energy with others. Give them the lift they need. Let each and every member on your team know how *amazing* they are and *really mean it* when you tell them, and *they will act amazing*. They will begin to believe in the picture you present of them, and act like superstars.

With an attitude of vitality in the workplace, you can change the whole vibrancy of the space. Even on cloudy days, people will feel your sunshine. It takes a constant mental decision to do this. It is part of the job of being a goal maker. One must have the goal of a vibrant and exciting environment where people believe in them, and feel they can succeed.

As a sales manager and goal maker, you are responsible for creating this. No one else will do it for you. If you really want to accomplish goals you set out, it takes energy. *Vitality is created.* It can be a driving force towards the daily progress towards goals, and it makes for a sane and fun environment to work in.

Part of this formula is the make sure you validate all the successes as they happen. Cheer the success of a salesperson when they have made a sale. Spread the good news through the office that others are selling! Other sales people will adopt the idea that *people are buying*, and they can *sell more too*. The rage of '*demand*' will be created just from a little inspirational vitality and sunshine.

If you inspire this vitality in others, they will pass it on to others as well. Salespeople will pass on the energy to their customers and those customers will pass it on to others. It is a magic formula of goodness that people respond too. No one truthfully loves to hear bad news. They love to share things that excite them. Compare the difference in how someone tells the story of a funeral, and one who tells the story of the recent baseball game they attended where their team won! You will see the difference. There are far too few things sometimes in the world that *truly excite* people, so whenever you can make something exciting like a product or service, they will share it with others.

So vitality is *created*. It is a driving force for you as a sales manager, and a driving force that can inspire salespeople under your charge. It can also become a positively infectious attitude to all the others around you, including your customers. It is a necessary and basic ingredient to reaching goals as a goal maker.

Do you want to see goals met? Try just spicing it up with an infectious vibrant attitude peppered with irresistible vitality. Goals get reached because someone has the energy to create the motion towards them. This is the magic of the goal maker. It is a necessary ingredient for a sales manager to be able to inspire others to greatness. One needs to be able to get them to see they are great, and live up to that.

This is done through having vitality in the workplace. Moving around, rather than sitting at your desk. Inject the life into the environment with your interactions with others. This operating basis requires energy. Even if you do not feel it at first, just pretend. At first you may not feel you have it, but as you see things happen around you, you will get infected with the vitality of this magic. Vitality is a created commodity, and it starts with the sales manager.

Continuance of Success

One of the best courses of action in the daily operations of a sales manager is the collection and cataloging of successes. As a sales manager, one should have an assistant that has a regular part of their operations collecting success stories from former clients. Success builds upon success. In the beginning this may seem like an arduous and unimportant task. However, once one sees the magic the results can be intoxicating.

Work into your system of business to collect stories from your clients that share their positive experiences with working with your company and its people. Collect as many as you can throughout the daily activities of business. Have all the staff in the entire company seeking to gather success reports and stories. This information is pure gold.

One should ask every client that fills one out if it is okay to publish the story, report, etc and share their experiences with others. Some may not want you too, and that is okay, as they are still useful.

Once one has this trail of successes starting to flow in, then there are specific places to channel this information. For ones that are approved by the author to publish and make available, those can be used on all lines. For the ones that are not approved, we will call those limited publications to the staff of the company only.

Here are some of the best uses:

- *Advertising*
- *Internal posters*
- *Email newsletters*
- *Mailers*
- *Training materials*
- *Sharing with sales personnel*

- *Use in presentations with other customers*
- *Websites & blogs*

There can be many more uses for each of these, but let's take up this short list one by one:

ADVERTISING

Success stories and testimonials are a wonderful thing to include in print advertising, radio ads, and even television ads of all kinds. These definitely would need to be approved by the person who wrote them for them to be used, and many times a company may just use the first name and last initial of the person in the print versions.

These can be magical in adding creditability to your company or organization, and advertising is the first and best front line use.

INTERNAL POSTERS

If you have a showroom or a place where other customers are often waiting in, these stories can be an excellent way to create interest. Sometimes a car dealership may have to have someone wait while credit is checked or some other party needs to arrive, etc. Placing these on posters around the showroom, or in the waiting area are a great way to share the consumer confidence you your product and services, and this helps sales a lot.

EMAIL NEWSLETTERS

If your company is collecting email identities, using success stories in a news letter is another great way to share the current event of what is happening with your organization. It also serves as a reminder to those that are sitting on the fence of their decision to buy that you are a great company.

MAILERS

Direct mailing is always a great way to reach people. Some businesses do better with it than others. If you are using direct mailing as a campaign of any kind, including client testimonials and success stories is a great way to create interest.

TRAINING MATERIALS

I suggest that a special bound book be created and used internally with every company that includes a massive compilation of client testimonials and successes. There is no better way to communicate to new trainees the responsibility they have in forwarding and continuing the positive reputation of the company through their actions than by having them read what the former clients are saying about the business they are starting to work in. It builds confidence, and can be very inspiring to know they are joining a group that is helping so many people with their products. Make sure you show them all the best testimonials. These are invaluable for training staff.

SHARING WITH SALES PERSONNEL

The sales personnel in many companies sell the product, and never see the end result. So other department makes delivery on the product, or service, and the client long forgets to call the sales person back and share their successes. Collecting success stories and sharing them with the sales staff is invaluable in terms of building upon morale and confidence. Sales people need to know that they are having successes. Lack of this information often means they can get trapped in their failures of the moment when they run into a rough spot, and forget about the successes of the past or gain knowledge of the successes from those around them. They need to know the company is delivering good products that people are happy about, or they will at some point quit and give up.

USE IN PRESENTATIONS WITH CUSTOMERS

Former client testimonials are a no-brainer when it comes to new customer presentations. Showing them a ton of happy customers builds confidence. I recommend having these kinds of success stories lying around any internal showroom floor in nice books, and binders that they can go through. Have the stories worked into ever page of the presentation materials in use as well. Never let them escape the showroom without reading at least one or two former client testimonials in the presentation. These are gold.

WEBSITES & BLOGS

With websites and blogs these use of success stories and testimonials is equally invaluable. The beauty of the online presence is that one can include as many as one wants without the concern of printing costs. Work them into daily or weekly blog posts. Work them into articles. Keep a running RSS feed of customer and client success stories streaming down one side or your website or blog as customers find you. Tie it in with all the photography of your products and services. There are literally countless ways to promote these testimonials online, just let your website designers go crazy with it.

BROAD USE OF SUCCESS STORIES & TESTIMONIALS

Testimonials and success stories are good news and good information that needs to be shared widely a broadly. Make sure you business is collecting them, and using them in all forms of advertising, and make sure the sales people get a chance to read them as well. There is no greater bullet to shoot through the armor of uncertainly than a well written former client testimonial. It melts the sales resistance, and helps to go a long way to removing any uncertainty about working with your company.

Abundance & Scarcity

    I have been in sales since I was a little kid, from the times when my mother and father would have me involved in school and Boy Scout fundraising drives to sell things to raise money for one cause or another. I sold everything from chocolate bars, to breakfast tickets and flowers. They did this with all the kids in my family, so it no wonder that at least one of us got involved in some sort of a sales profession.

    There is a particular law of life that I have learned through hard won experience over the many years of being involved in sales. This is the law of abundance versus scarcity. Whenever there is an abundance of something, one can feel free to consume as much as one wants without a concern when one wastes one or two. When there is a scarcity, the thought of wasting one or two is frightening.

Let's take an example of food. Whenever there is an abundance of food around, one can feel free to eat as much or as little as they want, and throw away unused food, even though it might only be slightly damaged, simply because there is abundance and having more food for tomorrow is not a concern. When food is scarce, and everyone probably has had an experience somewhere in their life when it was, one tends to save food, and if it is slightly bad, just cut out the bad parts and use the remainder. Also one cuts back on food consumption, and tries to make every crumb stretch, because food is scarce, and there is a panic or desperation that accompanies this scarcity. I will give you an example.

One time as a young man I was on a back packing trip that took us into the wilderness that was ten or fifteen miles from nowhere. On the first night I was there, squirrels or some other animals got into my pack over night and ate about half of the food I brought. The next day it rained, and even more of my food and clothes got soaked. Suddenly my planned food for the trip had gotten very scarce. I had two more days ahead of me before I could come home, and so a panic set in and I had to eat some food that I would not have ordinarily eaten, because I was desperate.

This same type event happens often in sales. Whenever you have an abundance of customers, it is easy to get comfortable and even waste a few bad apples. Whenever you have a scarcity of customers, one tends to work with people that you really should not, but you are only doing so because you are desperate. Working with a desperate frame of mind only leads to trouble.

So the key for anyone involved in sales is to apply the *law of abundance*. Always promote, and market yourself even when times are abundant, and you will always be free to choose from your lot the best customers and discard the difficult or problematic ones. If you get lax on your promotion when times are good, a period of scarcity will eventually follow, and you may soon find yourself working with customers that are living nightmares for you, and you will beat yourself up trying to survive with a horrible deal because you are desperate.

So whenever I find myself feeling like things are

scarce, I promote like crazy. Whenever I find things are in abundance, I still promote like a steady conductor at an orchestra. The key is to always promote. This gives me an abundance, and freedom to waste a few bad apples now and then.

This is a vital skill for a sale manager to understand when instructing others. Too often the sales person they are working with gets into a frame of mind that they cannot lose a customer because there are so few! The right connection to make as a manager is that this sales person needs to explore and expand their leads. In this case, they need be sat down at their desk or work station with the sales manager and go through all of their leads in recent weeks.

"What happened to this person?" one should ask. "What about this person?" "When was the last time you called so and so?" "What about this file here?" Keep doing this drill with them over and over again until they have a change in viewpoint. At some point they should flip out of that 'scarcity' frame of mind, and return to a busy productive frame of mind. Suddenly they will discover that their phone starts to ring again and lo and behold there are many other customers to work with. Then this rotten troublesome sales cycle they are involved in does not seem as vital, and they can withdraw from that customer awhile without feeling they are losing an opportunity.

It is all a matter of changing ones viewpoint, and getting so they can get re-focused. With the millions of people in the world today, no sales person should feel they are ever in a scarcity of prospects. However, this does happen and a sales manager needs to be able to recognize when they see a salesperson that is desperate to be able to tackle the matter with them immediately and facilitate this change of viewpoint.

It actually can become a wonderful game to be able to spot the troubles another does not see immediately in themselves, and they will often at some point laugh with realization on what corner they had boxed themselves into. However, with some it can be a longer process and they may need this drill repeated on them on weekly basis to be able to finally adjust their frame of mind in regards to abundance and scarcity.

The internet in our modern age makes scarcity an easier thing to tackle in some respects, but one can also get lost in it as well. It is not so much to have a salesperson answer his or her email, or send follow up messages. They need to break out of their rut and pick up the phone repeatedly over and over again until they get a live person and on then can they get the feeling of abundance rolling again after some repetition.

The Impact of a Negative Client

"There are only two types of customers: Ones *we want to have*, and ones *we want our competition to have*."

One can sometimes encounter a very, very nasty customer that insists on doing business with you or one of your salespeople. Over the years, when you deal with a lot of different customers and clients, you are bound to experience this from time to time.

A long time ago I learned some basic truths in sales. One particular truth is that sometimes your lines feel clogged. Whenever one has to deal with a particularly negative client, it is quite easy to feel this way. A black shadow lies across your soul, and you regret trying to face your daily routine. In real estate a sales transactions can last for weeks or months, so having a negative client on your communication lines can become quite taxing at times.

Occasionally I find I have to re-learn the lesson of being willing to let people walk and go on their way. If you have been in sales, at some point you may have encountered that feeling of grinding away with a really unpleasant client and getting nowhere. Ever run in to a person that eats up your time and in a general sense is a 'yucky' person?

I had one of those people on my lines once that lasted fo several weeks, and I took time to write down this chapter to communicate while it was still fresh. I had driven three times to show a particular lady a house that was an hour away from me, spending hours with her between appointments, on the phone and email.

I eventually was successful in getting her to write an offer and submit it on a Monday. She insisting on writing a garbage low ball offer which I did not feel right about submitting, but the listing agent was a good friend, and I was certain that a deal could eventually be negotiated.

Then the following day on Tuesday, while we were waiting for a response she called me and decided to cancel her offer because she had not heard from me immediately according to her schedule with an update. This was after I explained carefully to her the evening before that we would know anything until Wednesday as per the terms of the contract, and I would give her a call as soon as the listing agent got back with me with a response.

She became very incredibly ugly to me, hammered on me about 'her schedule for the process' and I suddenly stepped back and realized she had been quite ugly throughout the entire process. As she was blazing away at me on the phone with a negative attitude, I realized that I had been feeling quite out of spirits since I first started working with her. It was in a split moment that I made a decision based on optimum survival.

I decided that rather than try to spend more hours explaining to her and handling her self-generated and created upset, and try to make peace with her once again, that I would just clean the lines and cut her loose. I canceled her contract immediately without question, mailed her earnest money back and graciously terminated any agreements she had with me.

I cleaned the lines. What was the result? In the next few days I got to work with other happier clients and got two houses pending, and also a commercial building that I had been working on. I also rounded up a new great property listing! All of that happened seemingly almost within 72 hours of cutting Miss Yucky from my communication lines.

All these new clients were happy to work with me! Life was good again! For two weeks I had ground away with this really yucky person who was eating up all my time and was very critical of Realtors in general, and I did no other business. Immediately when I cleaned the lines and cut her loose, I found fresh deals flowing in and life was great again.

So sometimes it really pays to step back and clean the lines, and move on to fresh clients who respect you as a professional and really want to do business with you. Some people out there are just generally unhappy, yucky people that live miserable lives by their own choosing, but it does not have to be your choice too.

So whenever you as a sales manager or a sales person are working with a client that is overbearing and negative, remember you can always cut them loose. Sometimes it is for the better health of all concerned that you do this. Trying to hang onto and coddle a generally negative person who lives to make others miserable will only dampen the spirits of the individual working with them, and ultimately lose other business from the dark cloud they put over everything.

Learn to cut free from such people, and you will soon find there are many others you would rather work with. Learn to spot this in sales people you work with as well, because it is a matter of prosperity for the entire group that you do this.

It become an essential training skill for a sales manager to not only spot this situation and deal with it, but also to identify a particular sales person who you may have on your team that has a particular knack for attracting this type of client and muddying up the lines. One should never entirely rule out that it is exclusively the random client or customer that floats on the lines, and creates havoc.

Sometimes a member of your own team could be attracting them or has a referral source that is feeding this type of clientele to them. It can happen that an outside referral line is attracting these negative clients, and is 'referring' them to your team for a finder's fee when in fact they are sending your sales person their garbage customers they never want to do business with themselves.

There is a rule I have learned over the years that should be etched in stone on the wall in front of every sales manager's desk. It reads:

"There are only two types of customers: Ones *we want to have*, and ones *we want our competition to have*."

Think about that the next time you have one of those problematic and negative customers on your phone line, and make sure someone else is not also sending this type of client your way.

The Parachute Perspective

    As a goal maker, one sometimes creates a goal that just does not seem to suit. It may be that conditions in an activity or environment changed, and the goal no longer is a desirable one. To hang onto a goal and drive towards it because it was set and no other reason is not always going to end with a good result.

    Undesirable goals inspire no enthusiasm to accomplish, and thus it becomes daily drudgery to motivate anyone to pursue them. Just because someone with 'authority' authored the goal and ordered you to pursue it, does not mean that you should. Bad goals do exist, just like good ones. Sometimes they are made when not completely thought out, or before all the pertinent information was available to set it up correctly.

As a sales manager, one needs to have a 'parachute perspective' on being able to abandon unworkable goals. What is a 'parachute perspective'? It is the willingness to jump from the plane you are on and pull your parachute and head back to earth. Staying on a plane that is going nowhere is never going to be of any benefit. It is better to return to earth, get your feet planted squarely on the ground and set a new goal.

This parachute perspective embodies all areas of decision making as a sales manager. Sometimes one hires personnel that just do not fit in, no matter how one tries to inspire them. They have no ambition, no willingness to produce, and are merely riding the clock. Should one hold onto such a person on your team simply because the personnel department handed them to you as a resource? Certainly, one could do this, but it will make the going quite rough. Isn't it better to speak with the person and let them know that it is just not working out, and try to find their true goals in life and let them get on with it?

I once worked with a salesperson that just was not ambitious. He could not get into the spirit of production. After neglecting confronting him on this matter for months, knowing he was not happy, I finally had a conversation with him about this very point. I discovered that his real goal was to go to culinary school. He brightened up when he told me about his desires to become a chef, and own his own restaurant some day. Instead of beating him up about it, I helped him find his way into a culinary school in the following days, and even wrote him a letter of recommendation to the school to help him get accepted. This man had no business being on my sales staff. He was not a bad person, just an unwilling participant. In the end, he was happy, and so was I. I helped him get where he wanted to go, and he was following his dreams.

One needs to utilize the parachute perspective when experiencing situations like this, or any situation where a goal is stagnant and not moving despite all the efforts. Examine the situation and see if it is the right goal. With this salesman in the example above, becoming a successful salesman was not his goal. Why try to make it his goal? His goal was to become a chef!

Sure I could have given him a pep talk, and tried to inspire him to pursue it, as I have erroneously done with others in the past. It would have been to no avail, and he and I would have been miserable with the working relationship. He would be hating his job, and I would be miserable with his non-production and lack of daily enthusiasm. So I adopted a parachute perspective, and helped him jump from his current path and get on the right one for him.

This same thing can happen with monthly goals, quarterly goals and annual goals. I have experienced the complete lack of motivation from a sales staff in the past with the idea of meeting a financial quota for example. When I re-examined the goal with them, I found through survey that they could not get excited about looking at their deals as strictly dollar values.

What I discovered is that they could get excited about the number of orders sold. So I adjusted the quota to reflect number of orders, and made that the new goal. We arrived at the same end, but it became a goal they could embrace. They were inspired by a new viewpoint on the goal of getting a number of orders into customer's hands, rather than the goal of collecting a quota for income. The orders rolled in, and the money was still there.

This parachute perspective can span many areas of life. Sometimes one is involved in something in their personal life that is crossing over and complicating ones arrival at goals in their professional life. One needs to be able to examine both goals, and make sure they are desirable.

Sometimes one needs a new profession. Other times, one needs to bring to end relationship with another that is going nowhere. These decisions can be hard to confront sometimes. It takes courage, real courage to look at these things. It is never easy.

However, if one considers that happiness come with *pursuing goals* is connected to moving in a direction towards a desirable goal, it is vital. No one ever said life was easy. To take hold of a parachute, and jump from a path towards a goal that one has devoted so much time from can be a little scary. It is never easy to start over in a new direction. However, if one is ever to realize happiness, if is a necessary evil.

As a sales manager, helping others achieve goals is essential to daily operations. One must inspire them to reach personal professional goals. However, if one uncovers a situation where the person truthfully is on a path towards a wrong goal, it is a kindness to teach them about what is the nature of happiness, and this parachute perspective so that they can make their own decisions on what to do in regards to it.

If you can confront do this oneself, and help

others, then it makes that part of your job so much easier. One can also build a team of people around oneself that are truly moving in the same direction and together everyone on the team can achieve their share of greatness.

Charting Progress

Whenever one is following a goal, it always a good idea to chart the progress one makes towards it. No profession is easier to chart than the progress of sales. If one has a goal for example of one million in annual sales for a company, one would drawn a chart over the 12 months broken down into 52 weeks, and place it on the wall.

The best way to lay out one of these charts is to have a diagonal line drawn across the middle of the graph from beginning to end which become the 'goal line' for one to ideally follow through time to arrive at the final goal for the year.

With such as chart, one can start at zero sales on January 1st and One Million in sales on Dec 31st, and draw a grid with all the months in between and a diagonal line from zero to one million spanning across the year. See the illustration below:

These kinds of charts are best updated weekly, and one can see the progress as the year moves forward. Charts present more than just a visual progress, they also give one a sense of how things are going as one moves through the year. For example, in this illustration, one can see that the goal which is set is not being met halfway through the year.

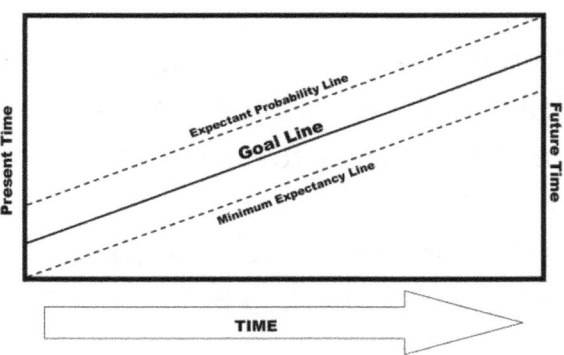

In this illustration, one can see that the goal that was set is being exceeded halfway through the year, and perhaps the sales manager needs to adjust the end goal and make it a little higher at some point.

One can also make smaller charts for individual weeks and months, and quarters along with the main one that is posted on the wall. Seeing the direction one is moving can alone be inspiring, and holding meetings in rooms with the charts are displayed can help the group take ownership for the progress as well.

The information should be shared with the sales team. It helps them with their own confidence, but also it helps them impart the confidence of the viability of the company to the customers they sell. Charting progress, and making the information known to the sales team is an essential ingredient to success, and leaves no mystery for others to guess at. One likes to know that the company they are working for is stable, expanding and progressive. These charts help to communicate this.

The charts also help a sales manager research the past, and easily see a time they need to research when things changed. One can see changes in the sales direction, and use the chart to research and go back and make adjustments. It is more like shooting in the dark for answers or grasping for straws in the hopes that one is lucky enough to make the right choice when one has no charts to refer to.

Charting progress helps one to see what is going

on, and use that information to improve the scene and continue expansion towards a goal.

Marketing & Goals

    Timing is everything in proper marketing. Marketing can be tied in with goals. How does one go about this? Once a sales manager sets goals for let's say the quarter in sales, and aligns them with the company goals, he or she should have some form of numerical target. This can be either a sales dollar volume quota, or the number or units sold, or some other quantitative measurement to determine when the goal is met. This is essentially your target to shoot for.

    Have you ever gone skeet shooting? If you try to shoot directly at a flying skeet with your gun, you will miss every time. The skill is being able to shoot in front of the where you expect the skeet to go, and time the meeting of the skeet with your buckshot. As a sales manager, one needs to be able to think into the future to anticipate and be ahead of the goal in order to make it happen. It is prediction, and adjusting for changes that makes one successful, as one never knows exactly where the skeet will go until it is launched.

One can do this with marketing. Whether one has direct control over marketing, or one has to work with another manager over that area, there should be collaboration between the two departments. Both should be flexible enough to work with each other and share common goals, as they are both interdependent on each other's success. Marketing has no funds to market without the income created by sales, and sales has no fresh influx of new leads if marketing is not working. Both have a stake in the game when it comes to cooperation on goals.

Let's say you have a lighting supply store that is selling retail items with a team of sales people on the floor. The business carries mostly lighting supplies, but also has some other cash and carry items people can buy that plug in that are not specifically lighting fixtures.

One plans out a marketing plan to include a sale at intervals throughout the year. Let's assume there is one sale for each quarter. These one could assume are fixed plans. A seasonal spring, summer, fall and winter sale is planned. However, no marketing plan should be too etched in stone. If one takes the example of the skeet shoot, the skeet is a moving target, and can shift unpredictably. So can life.

I will give you an example. When I was in Atlanta during the 1980's, I saw a shift in a lighting store that was a great example of such a move for their sales and marketing. In September 1989 hurricane Hugo hit the coast of South Carolina leaving 100,000 people homeless and even more without power. The entire State of South Carolina sold out of backup generators within days.

Some stores in South Carolina that had them were increasing prices by 5X and there was a lot of profiteering going on that was all over the news. Lighting stores in Georgia adjusted for this emergency, and pulled out all of their stocks of generators and created a huge sale to help Hugo victims.

Instead of focusing on point of purchase sales, they concentrated on donations and consigned a semi-truck to transport generators at no cost to give away to the victims of the storm. They did not jack up their prices, but sold in volume, and adjusted their fall marketing plan to this new development.

Most of the generators they sold at wholesale prices. Why would they do this? It was a brilliant marketing strategy is why. They helped victims of the storm, and sold the generators at cost without a profit through donations, and gave them away for free. Thousands of people came into the store that week to help make donations.

Do you think that many people simply came into the store and merely spent money only on that? Of course not, they also made other purchases while in the store. The store received a lot of good publicity on the radio for this good will gesture, and at the same time increased their traffic as a byproduct of this. Do you want to bet that sales manager met his or her quota that month? I visited this store, and made a donation myself. I also picked up some other items I needed for the home that I had been putting off at the same time. How many hundreds of other customers did the same?

This store could have ignored the disaster, and carried on with the fixed marketing plan in place and had sales on other items. However, by being able to be adjustable with their marketing plan, and adjusting for the news event, they not only helped thousands of people without power in a neighboring State, creating good will for the company, they also achieved their sales goals silently by making the adjustment.

Now, one can say this is *capitalizing on a disaster*, and question their morality. Of course there could be much debate on this, however, I spoke with the sales manager directly and the motivation was sincere and they were in shock as we all were and wanted to help these people. There was nothing immoral about it. In fact, before the sale even started the store took over 200 generators off the shelf and donated them without any cost and this truck was already en route before the sale hit the news lines.

It does not take a disaster to adjust marketing, however. Stores do this all the time, and smart sales managers plot out with their marketing managers plans for the quarter, and annual marketing, but make them adjustable. One cannot predict a hurricane in a neighboring State that will hit in September when doing their annual plans in December of the prior year. Nor can one predict the sudden blizzard, tornadoes, hail storms, ice storms, earthquakes, or any other type of natural disaster that can occur.

One cannot also predict political change that far

in advance. In the early 90's there was a sudden national rise in patriotism during the Gulf War that swept across the country during that time. You may remember that stores began stocking American flags, and other patriotic products and they sold in abundance. Somewhere a sales manager and marketing manager made the adjustment and took advantage of the change in political climate and boosted their sales.

Also in Atlanta during the early 1990's the Atlanta Braves baseball team achieved sudden and great popularity after years of mediocrity. Stores began stocking all kinds of MLB baseball products and 'Tomahawk' gimmicks all over town as the popularity grew. This is another adjustment that a wise sales manager or marketing manager makes.

I personally learned during this era that if you did not have the afternoon Atlanta Braves game playing on the radio in the showroom I was working in, that you could not keep people in the store long if they stopped in. Everyone was following the games on their car radio, home radios and even at work. If they stopped in for shopping during a game, you learned if you wanted them to stay in your store, *you better have the game on*. This was especially true if a spouse of a non-fan was dragging someone who was an avid fan along with them for shopping. Many times I had wives stop in and go out to their car to tell their husband to come in and look at the products telling them *'It's okay, they are listening to the game on in the store'* and they would come in. This is another example of adjusting for changes in environment.

Another example is when I was in New Orleans in 2011. The huge topic in that area was the oil spill off the gulf coast. The impact had made national news and was a mega-topic locally because of the lack of response from Washington and the damage it had on the local fishing industry. Local stores began stocking T-Shirts and other retail items concerning this issue, and one could not walk into a store in the French Quarter without seeing a reference to this incident. Sales managers of all the little stores were taking advantage of the local news event.

One learns that marketing plans need to be flexible when plodding down a course in a direction of a goal. Shifting sales and strategies to changes in the political or current news climate is essential to continuing the growth and progress towards your goals. One can also say that one needs to be alert for and in-tune with what is going on in the world around them as a sales manager, as well as think with this creative adjustment strategy whenever such events occur.

It is wisdom that one gains from practical experience in the role. Keep ones ears and eyes open to what is popular or timely in the world around one, and make adjustments in marketing to achieve your goals. If you can do this, you will often find a surprise boost now and again when you are least expecting it.

Envisioning Outcomes

Envisioning an outcome for oneself is an essential part of understanding the magic of goals. Sometimes as a sales manager, one can play a part in using imagination to create a reality which others play with and follow. In these situations, one can often set into motion events that one never predicted, but because one used imagination sought to inspire solely as a fundamental, it shares that energy with others. There is an old saying that '*A candle loses nothing by lighting*

another candle'. As a sales manager, one needs to remember this rule above all, and be there to help light another's candle when it is possible to do so.

The story of the '*Whomper*'

During the mid 1990's I was in Atlanta working as a Sales Manager. My business partner and I had set a weekly target to conform to our progress towards our monthly goal. At one point in the week, we were behind in sales for the week as a couple of big deals had been postponed until the following week. They in fact were in danger of rolling into the next month, and throwing off our task of meeting the goal we set.

I told Karen that I was going to throw up the '*Whomper*' in reference to the 1992 sailing movie 'Wind'. In this movie the character played by Jennifer Grey hoists a sail she designed and dubbed the 'Whomper' for use when they had fallen behind in the America's Cup Race. I told Karen, we need one big sail to get us back on track and into the race. A few days later after making this challenge I managed to pull off an unexpected big sale, and saved the sales stats for week. I accomplished through first imagining the outcome, and then chasing that vision.

After that we began calling any big sale a 'Whomper' and often saying that someone needed to throw up a 'Whomper' or some similar statement. Karen would often jovially go around the office holding her arms wide saying *'Whomp', 'Whomp', Whomp'* over and over again when we were close to breaking a goal. It was all in good fun, and it created a *'game within a game'* in our weekly sales activities. Everyone wanted to pull off a big sale, and many times they did so as could be expected when one lights such a candle.

I include this story here in this book as it relates to the purpose of goals. When one can get the fever going in a sales office about reaching a goal, anyone can play and will play. It becomes a group activity of creation, and the outcome is always therapeutic. Goals do not have to be some lofty 'high up on the mountain' sort of objective. They can be, but one also needs the short term goals and games to make the larger ones a reality. Frequently it is these smaller successes that become the most memorable.

The story of the Cowboy

Another example of goal setting on a smaller level has to do with an individual setting a pre-determined outcome for a sale in their own mind, and then seeking to make it a reality in the world. I had a conversation with my showroom sales manager once about a beautiful Art Deco stained glass lamp that we had just received in a recent shipment. We had just unpacked it, and finished setting up the display and were admiring the artistry of the product. It has a statue of a reclining nude on a tree branch that had a magnificent stained glass lamp shade which represented the leaves in autumn colors. The coloring was exquisite and it was the highest priced piece on our showroom, so we had a set up a special display for it all by itself.

In this conversation, my showroom manager Phil said determinedly "I am going to sell this lamp". As we continued to talk, he further explained *"The buyer is going to be a cowboy, and he is going to come in before Christmas and I am going to sell him this lamp. You wait and see."* Upon hearing this, other sales people in the area who heard him say this as well began to joke, and this made him even more determined to make his predetermined sale a reality. It was early December, and I had thought this was all in good fun and secretly wanted him to be a success at this to make the other non-believers eat their words.

We sold a lot of lamps in the coming weeks because of the holidays, but as we approached the final week of Christmas Eve, this special lamp still had not been purchased. I was beginning to think that it would not sell, and that it was going to be with our showroom a long time as it was too expensive for the local buyers. All sorts of things start to cross one's mind to try to justify a non-sale of such a beautiful product, and I was no exception. I thought that it might just become our showroom feature that helped sell other less expensive lamps, etc.

When the day before Christmas Eve finally came, I was working the showroom with Phil and one other salesperson. We had seen a lot of last minute shoppers that day, and sold a lot of inventory. This beautiful sculptured lamp was still there, unsold. During a slight lull in the flow of customers, Phil and I were sitting at a desk adding up and sorting out a pile of receipts, and a bell rang indicating someone had come into the front showroom. I looked up, and there was a tall man wearing a cowboy hat and boots looking around the showroom. It was surreal. I looked at Phil, and he looked at me, and said *"There is my customer"* and proceeded to go out to greet him with a determined look on his face.

Now one must realize that we had already broken sales records this season for our lamp sales, and the past few days we had made an unprecedented number of sales. We still had a lot of inventory, and other customers came in behind the cowboy too.

Before proceeding out to help the other customers, the other salesperson on duty and I exchanged glances, and proceeded to try to be a fly on the wall as Phil tried to fulfill his destiny on this sale while we were working with other customers. Phil showed this man every lamp in the showroom and was with him for almost a full hour, and then finally brought him around to the big one, the Art Deco sculptured beauty. The man was impressed, and Phil continued to talk to him, pitch him on the merits of this one above all others, etc. I and the other salesperson sat at desks after wrapping smaller sales with the other customers, and hovered nearby just listening, but trying not to act as if there was anything other than routine business going on.

I wish I could say that Phil made this particular sale. That the outcome was perfect, and the man purchased the lamp he wanted him to. The cowboy was entertained, and did make a purchase, but not that lamp. We did not sell that particular lamp before Christmas, although one could argue that it inspired others who saw it to but ones of lesser value, and was therefore a great marketing tool. Eventually Phil did sell this lamp, although it was not to a cowboy specifically. If I recall correctly it was a lady who was a collector. Ironically she was from Texas, and she and her husband were Dallas Cowboy fans, so perhaps one could say Phil did achieve his desired outcome after all?

In any event, I include this story as it is a great example of how imagination can drive and inspire one to reach a goal. Had Phil not posed his own challenge to himself, and vocalized it to others around him, it perhaps would not have taken on a meaning. This personal goal became a daily game for himself during the holidays that season, and everyday he would begin by jokingly saying *'Today my cowboy is going to walk in'* and take on the challenge of the daily routine of sales. Playing a game, and wrapping it up with some imagination never hurt any salesperson.

The lesson here is that one needs to believe in oneself, the goals they set no matter how crazy or specific and make that vision a reality. The outcome may not be the exact reality that you perhaps painted originally, but if you believe in yourself and continue to work in that direction, the result can be greater than you envisioned. Phil not only eventually sold the lamp, albeit later than his designated target date, but in the process of trying to fulfill his imagination he made hundreds of sales for himself along the way. His drive for this goal he painted made for a harvest of other sales along his journey.

What was particularly interesting about this experience was that Phil's creative imagination inspired other salespeople to make similar challenges in future times. As new inventory would come in, a salesperson would invent the characteristics of an imaginary customer they were going to sell it to and tell others this was the outcome they were preparing to create. It was a remarkable and fun game, and the candle of Phil's idea lit the candle of many others. Such is the power of imagination.

The story of the 'Hammer'

Several years later I worked a job where I answered calls in a hotline which was designed to find prospects for a sales team. My job was to answer the hundreds of calls, and find out the persons needs and determine their qualifications for our company's services. If they were unqualified, we directed them to other resources. If they were qualified, we took down their information and arranged for a salesperson to call them back to go over more details and in all hope make a sale. If they sold the service to the prospect, I received a small commission.

One evening, I was working the late night shift, and determined that I had a workable prospect on the line to refer to a salesperson. The lady was grateful to have found what she was looking for, and I took down her information and arranged to have a salesperson call her back that evening. When I called the salesperson who was on duty, he answered and seemed a bit spiritually down as we spoke. He had had a rough day so far, and was tired. I told him, *"Don, I have a great lead for you. I know that you can make this sale, because you are 'the hammer' and 'the hammer' never misses"*. I imbued my message to him that he was the greatest, and that was why I chose to call him. He brightened right up, and took the information and called the woman. He indeed made the sale. A few days later I ran into his girlfriend at a store, and she said to me *"Oh, you should have seen Don that night! He was walking around the house saying 'I am the hammer' and puffing his chest up. I think you made a monster out of him"* she laughed.

So in this short phone call, I inspired this man to believe in himself to go forth and accomplish greatness. I told him he was great, and made sure he believed in it himself before I got off the phone with him. He made the call, and made his sale partially because he now believed in himself and also because he wanted to live up to this reputation that I had created within a few moments on the phone with him. He became this great salesperson who believed in himself, and set about the goal of closing the prospect in front of him.

So we find that goal making is not only done for a large group, but one also needs to recognize that an individual needs to have a goal. Imagination is a sales manager's best friend. Whenever one encounters a situation where things are dull, sticky or a salesperson does not believe in them, use your imagination and create a goal for them by inspiring them to believe in something. It never hurts to light the candle for someone and share your imagination for them, and many times they will embrace it and share this dream with others. *A candle loses nothing by lighting another candle.*

Goal making is a magic quality that comes from being able to envision the future, and the outcome one wants to see become a reality. Sometimes that reality can be different from what one projects, and that is completely okay. What is important is making the goal, using ones imagination and becoming that person they need to be to reach that goal. In the case of the 'Whomper' I know it became a game between me and others on the sales lines in that day to be 'the Whomper' and build their own legendary image among each other.

With the story of the cowboy, Phil so thoroughly believed in his imaginary customer, and the outcome, that he did eventually materialize this sale and many others as he sought hard to make this a reality for others to see. With the story of the 'Hammer' I made an image and imagined reputation for that salesperson and offered it up for him to grab hold of that ideal and he did so. It became his own creation that he wanted to achieve and live up to, and it helped him with many other sales as time progressed.

So a goal maker needs to help others imagine, create and embrace ideas and goals. They also need to help others envision the outcome, and let them get on with it if they are already doing it. Imagination in the workplace of a sales team can become infectious, and extremely fun. It makes the environment a happier one to work in, and turns 'work' into 'play'. Feel free to light another's candle with the spark of imagination.

Intention & the Goal Maker

Intention is what makes things happen. There is a huge difference between just 'doing something' and intending something to happen. Intention is the driving energy that makes it possible to do the impossible. Being in sales all of my life, I have to continue to remind myself of this. If I do not intend something to completion, it does not happen, even though I may be doing some of it.

The best arena to see the outcome of intention that I know is sports. It is easily apparent in the game of contest whether one team or player has intention, and the other doesn't. The ever famous story of Joe Namath in Super Bowl II is a good example of this. The other team was heavily favored to win, and Joe came out in the press in the prior week saying that his team was going to win, and he 'guaranteed it'.

Anyone hearing that thought he would eat his words, but with sheer intention, he did lead his team to victory on game day. Other famous examples are Babe Ruth, who as the story has it pointed his bat at the stands in the outfield prior to taking a swing, and then hit a home run into the very section of the stands endearing himself with baseball fans from there on as a legend of the game. Intention is what makes things happen.

Have you ever watched the highlight clips of Barry Sanders, the Detroit Lions most famous running back? It is hard not to marvel at his unstoppable intention in the way he played. His highlight films are so amazing in the world of athletics, and it is a perfect example of the power of intention.

In buying or selling a home or any product, it is the same thing. If you have intention, you can get it done. If you really intend to sell a home, you can get it done. If you really intend to buy a product, you can get it done. No matter the obstacles that may be in the way, intention is what makes things happen. If you do not have it, you leave you life in the hands of 'chance' or 'luck' and odds are you won't make it. Intention is what makes things happen.

What a sales manager must be able to gain skill in is teaching his or her salespeople this lesson about intention. Of course, one must first understand it themselves. It is the driving magical force that they have within themselves alone to make things happen in spectacular fashion. To be without it is to just coast along, and drift with the hopes of random success. If one has it, it is the difference between a soft gentle breeze behind a sail boat and a controlled hurricane. Intention is the controlled hurricane on how great things happen.

Intention is the driving force of a successful salesperson, and it is the sales manager that knows and understands this that can drive this concept into those that he or she leads. It also is an essential ingredient in achieving goals. It is not just important enough to draw up some lofty goals, paste them on a wall and throw around some praise and 'rah-rah' and hope those goals will be met. No, one has to drive the goal home with focused *intention*. This is the hammer to the nail. It is what makes goals a reality in the physical universe.

If one really wants to understand the subject of goals, and being the best goal maker they can be, one must know in their heart that intention is the driving force. It is the difference between asking someone to produce, and doing so with warm energy and spiritual electricity compelling them to produce. *Intention compels.*

Intention sometimes has to be demonstrated by the sales manager in a hands-on operation to drive the point home. The lesson one is trying to get others to embrace is that they are champions of their own destiny. They are their own 'guiding force' and they are at the helm of their own ship, no matter how rough the seas. It is the viewpoint of placing someone in control, and letting them fully understand without a shadow of doubt that they are, and letting them do it.

Sometimes one needs to give them a real practical example. Get them to sit in a car or imagine themselves at the wheel of a great ship. Tell them to grab the steering wheel. Let them know that they are in rough seas and that they must save all on board or die trying. Try to get them to imagine this image, and perhaps through the power of imagination they can taste the sensation of 'it all depends on their actions'.

One can also get the person to recall a moment in

their life that was similar to that which you are asking them to imagine. Get them to not focus on the lack of control, or any disaster or negative thing that may have happened. No, get them to remember the moment that they realized they could do something about it. This is the first step to them understanding intention. It comes from deep within. It is sort of a driving determination that some call 'intestinal fortitude'.

With everyone in your group focusing on the goals you set as a goal maker, and understanding intention, you can get any goal accomplished. It simply takes a majority of the group to have the real intention to make it happen. It may take a lot of one on one work, and empowerment from you to get them to see it, but it can happen.

You as a sales manager must also know and understand intention personally in order to make these goals become a reality. You are the one that they will listen to and follow if you have it. This is the secret to being a success as a goal maker, and sales manager.

There is an old expression that 'a candle loses nothing by lighting another candle'. Sometimes we find our inspiration from others by seeing their courage, and we find that somehow our candle is also lit with courage. As a sales manager, one must be the candle that lights the other candles with intention. When you can do this, you will fully understand the joy of being a goal maker.

Summary

In summary of what has been covered in this book, one learns that there are many aspects to being a goal maker. There is *leadership and teamwork*, and it becomes essential to know what they are. One cannot solely depend up the talents of a few individuals, but must be able to inspire and obtain production from all members of a team, as well as let all the team players participate.

One learns that there are many roles that a *sales manager* can play, but the most important of them all is that of the *goal maker*. This is what guides the group.

In this book we learned what *true happiness* is, and it is not the obtaining of goals themselves. It is the journey that creates the happiness in life and that sense of accomplishment as one continues to progress towards a goal that is the fabric of living.

As a sales manager, we also come to learn there are *different types of goals.* There are *long term goals, quarterly goals, short terms goals* and even *specialty goals.* All are important, but it is the smaller goals that drive the larger ones.

We learned that building teamwork can be done through *training and drilling*, and that these can be done as both an individual and a group activity. A well trained and drilled staff will help a sales manager see their goals realized. One also comes to realize that goals are driven by knowing that people are not limited, and have potential that can yet be realized.

We discover that is also important to keep an *open communication* between the sales manager and his sales team, and vice versa and also with the customer. One can use sales meetings to forward this as well. Open communication is essential to achieving goals, as well as making adjustments to them as one learns new things and times change.

We learned to break down what is truly

important in decision making, so as to continue towards and accomplish a goal. We also covered the value of following through and when it is necessary, one should have a *parachute perspective* and use it when necessary.

We also covered the importance of maintaining *harmony, honesty and trust,* creating *games* and inspiring others with *vitality* in the environment. We also looked at what it takes to be *resilient* as a sales manager, by taking care of oneself so one never loses energy or focus on the goals or their role as a goal maker.

We also addressed how a negative client can get on a salesperson's lines, and zap the energy and enthusiasm from them leaving them in a state of hopelessness. Also, salespeople can begin to feel there is a *scarcity* of clients, and the resolution is to make them aware of the *abundance* of other prospects that exist through a practical exercise. We also learned that we can reach new clients through a constant campaign of *sharing successes* of those who have come before them. One can also adjust their marketing plan to the changes in the times to boost sales and achieve goals as well.

Finally we examined the importance of

imagination and *intention* as it relates to a goal maker, and how this drives the entire activity. With intention, a goal maker can achieve anything they desire for the group they lead. With imagination, one can light the candle of others and let them become who they truly seek to be.

This summarizes the contents of this book. It is up to you now to use this with the sales people that you have in your charge, and make your dreams a reality.

Cheers!

Acknowledgements

Throughout the process of this book, and this series on the Art of Sales Management, have received much encouragement and inspiration from many places, which I include all as my friends and family.

I would like to especially thank my sister Jeanne, and my brother Bob for taking time to give their opinions on countless cover designs, and concepts.

I would like to thank my friends Phil, Amanda, Allison, Tim, Sue and Jeff for just being there to bounce ideas off of.

I especially would like to acknowledge all the great sales managers who were amazing goal makers that I ever had the pleasure to work alongside. Among some of those greats were Dan, Owen, Juana and Marissa in all the various companies and organizations I have ever worked for.

Then there are all the wonderful sales people who I have had the pleasure of serving as their sales manager over the years who were such an inspiration in their daily dedication, and whom it was a sheer joy and excitement to be a part of their careers.

Once again I acknowledge my wonderful wife Margarita for all her tireless review of my work, and encouragement. She has inspired me over the years to become a goal maker probably more than most. I love you honey!

Finally, I cannot close a book on the subject of being a goal maker without mentioning my brother-in-law Dwight Matheny, who passed away in 2011. He was one of the greatest goal makers I ever had the pleasure of working alongside, and the people's lives and communities that he touched are a credit to his legacy and memory to this day. You will never be forgotten my friend.

About the Author

Michael Delaware is a Phoenix, Arizona native who now resides in Battle Creek, Michigan with his wife Margarita. He also lived in Georgia for 15 years in the 1980's and 1990's where he owned and operated a stained and beveled glass studio in the Metro-Atlanta area. During those years he was an active volunteer in the community, coordinating annual Arts and Crafts Festivals in the downtown district of Roswell, Georgia. He also participated in Arts & Crafts Shows for over 25 years as a vendor in numerous States. He has been a Michigan resident since 1999.

His other published works include numerous

non-fiction books on real estate, sales management, marketing and other self-help topics. He has also published fiction and non-fiction stories for children

As an illustrator and photographer, he has included his works in his own books and blogs. He enjoys hiking and mountain biking in the great outdoors and taking long walks in the woods with his dog.

Currently he is an active Realtor in Michigan and frequent community volunteer. He is a member of the National Association of Realtors, The Council of Residential Specialists, and the Michigan Association of Realtors. He is also an active member of the Battle Creek Area Association of Realtors where he was awarded *'Realtor of the Year'* in 2010, and served as Board President in 2011. He founded his own independent publishing company in 2012.

To follow Michael:

www.MichaelDelaware.com

Facebook.com/MichaelDelawareAuthor

Linkedin.com/in/MichaelDelaware

@MichaelDelaware

Other titles by the author available as eBooks:

The Art of Sales Management: Lessons Learned on the Fly (also available in print)

The Art of Sales Management: 75 Training Drills to Build Confidence, Excellence & Teamwork

Small Business Marketing: An Insider's Collection of Secrets

Arts & Craft Shows: The Top 10 Mistakes Artist Vendors Make... And How to Avoid Them!

Arts & Craft Shows: 12 Secrets Every Artist Vendor Should Know

Inspiration: The Journey of a Lifetime

For Real Estate:

Understanding Land Contract Homes: In Pursuit of the American Dream

Land Contract Homes for Investors

Going Home... Renting to Home Ownership in 10 Easy Steps

In Children's Fiction:
Scary Elephant Meets the Closet Monster

In Children's Non-Fiction:
My Name is Blue: The Story of a Rescue Dog

More titles will be available in print in late 2013 and in 2014. For a current list of available print books visit:

www.ifandorbutpublishing.com

If you enjoyed this book, don't overlook reading the first book in this series:

Available at major bookstores everywhere, and also through the publisher's website:

www.ifandorbutpublishing.com

The Art of Sales Management

 The Art of Sales Management series has a special website and blog that covers more information about forthcoming books, events and a new forum for discussion is coming soon in 2014.

 You can find the website here:

 www.artofsalesmanagement.com

www.ingramcontent.com/pod-product-compliance
Lightning Source LLC
LaVergne TN
LVHW011417080426
835512LV00005B/119